Spot the difference! (shop assistant at Patricia Field, Fabulous!)

Ear ring, VB-style

My surprise trip to the Ritz in Paris: Coco Chanel Suite. Just fabulous. David took the pictures (see below)

I always like to go for a natural kind of look!

I told you I had bad spots!

Playtime: vintage shopping at What Goes Around Comes Around in New York

Sex and the sushi

I always go for a less conservative look when having dinner in Paris!

Will my bum look big in these?

'Victoria is someone who makes high fashion relevant for everyone. She has really brought fashion into the mainstream and brought awareness to designer fashion that would not have been possible without her. Not only does she love fashion but she really understands it and how it works best for her. Victoria is not just a fashion icon; she is an icon full stop.'

ROLAND MOURET

Victoria Beckham

that extra half an inch

with Hadley Freeman

PHOTOGRAPHY BY ELLEN VON UNWERTH

Still-life photography by Benoît Audureau Illustrations by Cecilia Carlstedt

MICHAEL JOSEPH
An imprint of Penguin Books

MICHAEL JOSEPH

Published by the Penguin Group
Penguin Books Ltd, 80 Strand, London WC2R 0RL, England
Penguin Group (USA) Inc., 375 Hudson Street, New York, New York 10014, USA
Penguin Group (Canada), 90 Eglinton Avenue East, Suite 700, Toronto, Ontario, Canada M4P 2Y3
(a division of Pearson Penguin Canada Inc.)
Penguin Ireland, 25 St Stephen's Green, Dublin 2, Ireland (a division of Penguin Books Ltd)
Penguin Group (Australia), 250 Camberwell Road,
Camberwell, Victoria 3124, Australia (a division of Pearson Australia Group Pty Ltd)
Penguin Books India Pvt Ltd, 11 Community Centre, Panchsheel Park, New Delhi – 110 017, India
Penguin Group (NZ), 67 Apollo Drive, Mairangi Bay, Auckland 1310, New Zealand
(a division of Pearson New Zealand Ltd)
Penguin Books (South Africa) (Pty) Ltd, 24 Sturdee Avenue,
Rosebank, Johannesburg 2196, South Africa

Penguin Books Ltd, Registered Offices: 80 Strand, London WC2R 0RL, England

www.penguin.com

First published 2006
1

Text copyright © Moody Productions, 2006
Portrait photography © Ellen Von Unwerth, 2006
Still-life photography © Benoît Audureau, 2006
Illustrations © Cecilia Carlstedt, 2006

The credits on p.308 constitute an extension of this copyright page

Set in Bodini and FirminDidot
Art directed, designed and typeset by Nikki Dupin
Colour reproduction by Dot Gradations Ltd, UK
Printed and bound in Italy by Graphicom, srl

A CIP catalogue record for this book is available from the British Library

ISBN-10: 0–718–14991–2
ISBN-13: 978–0–718–14991–8

TO MY MUM

My first fashion guru, who taught me to sew, showed me
how clothes should fit and who told me never to wear
horizontal stripes and never to eat beetroot because it stains

And most importantly, she taught me to enjoy being a girl

(P.S. Jacks may have brought me up but in actual fact I know
that my real mother was Joan Collins – but that must
always remain a secret. Mum's the word...)

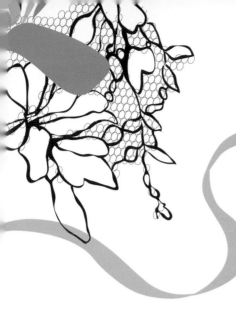

CONTENTS

Shoe by Christian Louboutin

introd

uction

THERE ARE PEOPLE OUT THERE WHO ONLY WEAR CLOTHES 'BECAUSE YOU HAVE TO' OR 'BECAUSE IT'S COLD'. BE WARNED: THIS BOOK IS NOT FOR THEM!

IT'S FOR GIRLS WHO LOVE FASHION. WHO LOVE THAT MAGICAL TRANSFORMATION OF MATERIAL ON A HANGER INTO SOMETHING THAT MAKES YOU WANT TO TWIRL IN FRONT OF A MIRROR, that gives you the confidence to think: You know what? I look great! Fashion is how we express our personalities. Our way of saying, 'This is who I am,' sometimes even, 'This is who I would like to be.' Most of all, fashion is about having fun and using your imagination.

I have no qualifications to write this book other than a lifelong passion which, combined with the extraordinary way in which my life has turned out, has given me the chance to wear some amazing clothes, meet some amazing people – and learn a hell of a lot along the way. And this is what I hope to share with you: the passion, the insight and the tips.

First, I'd like to knock a few things on the head. The idea that, once you have a bit of money, you start staggering around wearing couture and stilettos all day long, is as mad as thinking you'll be living on caviar and champagne. The staples remain the same whatever happens in your life. Toast is still my favourite food and, at the

My favourite shoes: Christian Louboutin for Roland Mouret

In the early years I always used to push a different kind of look...

end of the day, jeans are probably what I'm happiest wearing. (As proof, jeans were the first thing I set my sights on designing. If I was a cook I'd probably be perfecting the ultimate toaster.) Looking good isn't about money, it's about style. And style never goes out of fashion.

Designers borrow from the street, they borrow from the past, and there's no copyright on that; the genius of the greats – designers or individuals – lies in the way they put it together, and I feel incredibly privileged to talk to these people about their influences and their techniques. You'd be surprised to learn how many ideas come from history, whether it's a hundred years ago or thirty. Second-hand doesn't mean second class, as anyone who has discovered vintage shops will know.

My own inspiration comes from fashion icons of the last century: Grace Kelly, Jackie Onassis and my muse-for-all-seasons, Audrey Hepburn. *Breakfast at Tiffany's* must be my favourite movie of all time, and you could still wear anything from that today. And what do these women have in common? Simplicity. The understanding that it's all about shape – not just body shape, but the silhouette: the hat, the sunglasses, the bag, the shoes. Looks that have staying power.

My image, if you like, began at my stage school, where it was drummed into us that grooming was everything: nails, hair, make-up, it all had to be perfect if you wanted to get that job. In those pre-Spice Girls days, I was simply Victoria Adams. 'Posh Spice' came about because of how I looked: the bob, the heels, the little black Gucci dress. Except that it wasn't Gucci. It was Miss Selfridge, and I've still got it, though it finally fell to bits from being worn to death. But other things from that time – ten years ago now – I can and do still wear. For example, a Dolce & Gabbana little tube dress in a beautiful narrow pinstripe with built-in corset – the first corset dress I ever bought. 'Buy cleverly' and things will last. Remember: nothing is more expensive than the thing you only wear once.

Apart from when I'm doing fashion shoots for work (where the clothes are planned), I never use a stylist, never have and never will. Why let somebody else have all the fun? I decide what I'm going to wear and it's been that way since I was fourteen, when my mum let me loose in C&A. She, of course, was my first fashion guru, with a strict list of do's and don'ts. Geri of the Spice Girls had her own, one of which I will never forget: don't let it all hang out. If it's your legs that are on display

– like in a miniskirt – put those boobs away. Whereas if you're wearing trousers, then you can get away with something a bit plunging. Fashion is about feeling sexy, not inciting a riot.

A lesson that anyone can learn from just walking down the street, is to know your limitations. Other people's mistakes are easy to spot. So if your thighs aren't your best feature, then choose your jeans carefully: different cuts flatter different shapes, and there are loads of styles out there. I know; I've investigated them. If the idea of wearing a size 14 freaks you out, don't try to squeeze into a 12; buy the size that fits and cut out the label. Life's challenging enough, why be challenged by your clothes? Not that I haven't made mistakes. The most cringe-making was when David and I turned up wearing identical leather outfits (Gucci) at a Versace party . . . Not clever from any perspective. Keep your eyes open and your instincts intact – and those old enough to remember should never forget Dorian of *Birds of a Feather*...

From as far back as I can remember, I was always on the fashion road. At school I studied textiles for GCSE and my great claim to fame was starting the trend of wearing one pair of socks pushed down on top of another! But when I met the girls, my life took a bit of a detour. Now, with my various design projects up and running, I'm doing something I'd probably have ended up doing anyway, fulfilling a dream which I now realize that I have had for ever.

I'm not a six-foot-tall model, nor am I a pin-up for men, and, for this book, that's my strength, because I'm a girls' girl. In most respects I am very ordinary: smaller-boned than average, perhaps, but normal height, normal face, normal hair: the girl-next-door who got lucky. However nowadays it's hard for me to shop like I used to – popping in every week to see what was new on the rails – though the high street is still my first choice for basics. What's been great for me in writing this book is that it's given me the opportunity of getting back into that groove, my sister, Louise, being my chief scout, bringing out armfuls of stuff to Madrid from all my favourite shops, plus investigating a whole raft of new shopping options, including supermarkets. And these days, even when you live abroad as I do, you can always buy online. But wherever it comes from, every single thing I mention in this book has been chosen for the simple reason that it works; and if something doesn't work, then I'll say that too.

I have never lost that excitement of trying on new clothes, the bedroom looking

Victoria clearly loves fashion, and her style is watched and copied by many. It's interesting to me to look at how her personal style has evolved over the years

MATTHEW WILLIAMSON

like a jumble sale, remembering a pair of shoes in the back of the wardrobe that will pull a look together, finding a new top that will reinvent something I've had for years. I meet people who are so cool they could freeze your hand, whereas I still get excited when I'm lucky enough to be sent amazing pieces – like the Prada bag which I have used virtually every day since it arrived, doubling as everything from hand luggage to a pillow. But, if I'm being honest, the buzz is no different when I come across a great little find in the market or a vintage piece.

I've come a long way in the last ten years, but this book is not my attempt to tell you what or what not to do, it's just to share some of what I have learned, from tips from the best make-up artists and hairdressers, to the difficult (but not impossible) task of cramming nappies and baby bottles into a little Fendi bag. As for the title, I'm actually talking about high heels. OK, so it's a bit tongue-in-cheek – but that's what it's all about. And as every woman knows, that extra half an inch makes all the difference...

Shoe by Gucci

As for the title, I'm actually talking about high heels. OK, so it's a bit tongue-in-cheek – but that's what it's all about

Jeans

Jeans by VICTORIA BECKHAM for ROCK & REPUBLIC, LEVI'S RED TAB, ACNE JEANS, SASS & BIDE and SERFONTAINE

JEANS ARE THE OBVIOUS PLACE TO START. THEY HAVE BECOME NOT JUST THE BACKBONE BUT SPINAL CORD, RIBCAGE AND, FOR SOME OF US, THE WHOLE SKELETON OF A WOMAN'S WARDROBE.

SO IT'S A REAL JOLT TO THINK THAT THIS HAS REALLY ONLY BECOME THE CASE IN THE PAST DECADE OR SO. Remember how bad they used to be in the 80s and 90s? Unflattering, and almost always with that hideous tapered cut that makes everyone look like they have drumsticks for legs. Definitely the less-cool element of 80s fashion.

But, in the past decade, jeans have become hugely important in women's wardrobes and it's hard to think back to how we coped without them. I mean, what would we wear when going straight from work to a cool bar in the evening? Or when playing with the kids in the park without having to worry about looking frumpy or getting our clothes dirty but still wanting to look half-good? I honestly can't remember. No other piece of clothing can be worn in so many, and such different, situations and always look good.

Jeans have always had a chequered history in the cool stakes. When they were invented, they were just there to provide sturdy clothes for hard-working cowboys out on the plains. It was really in the 50s that they became cool – when

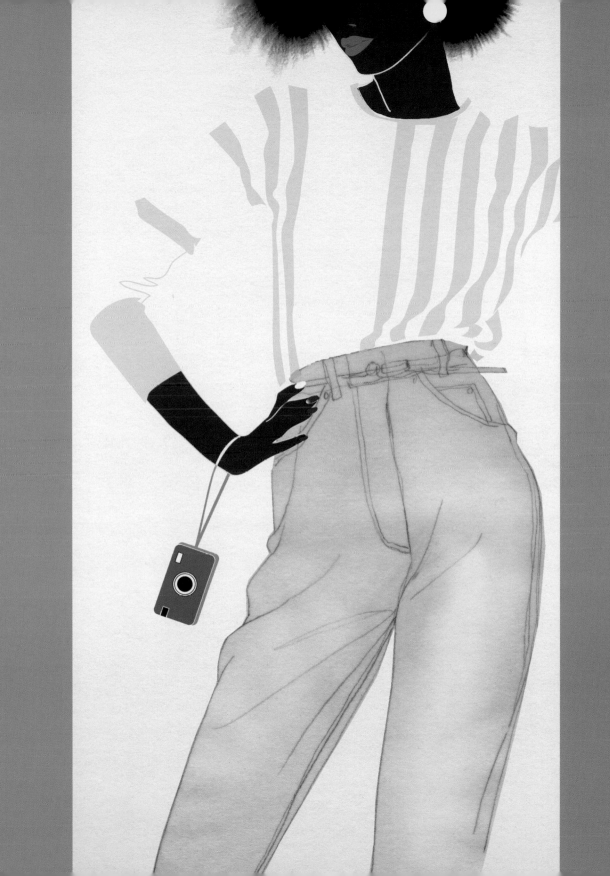

A Silver Jeans factory in Canada, 1921

James Dean hooked his finger through his denim belt loop, instantly making them the symbol for sexy teenage rebellion – and original Levi's Red Tab are now real collectors' items. But jeans became so common, and so badly made, it was inevitable that they would then languish by the 80s. Nowadays they are made to complement a woman's figure and it's hard to imagine they'll ever fall out of fashion's favour again.

And even though I do love getting dressed up, everyday clothes do have to be practical. There's always the risk of baby sick down my front and that's why I pretty much live in jeans and T-shirts – jeans are flattering but easy to just throw in the washing machine and T-shirts, as every mum knows, are great for mopping your children's noses.

Best of all, there is no age limit on jeans. A sixty-five-year-old granny could wear jeans and she'd look good, as long as it was a pair that suited her shape. That is something to bear in mind: we all change shape as we get older and so you'll almost certainly need to change the style of jeans you wear every few years instead of automatically still buying the same sort you were wearing when you were twenty-one. That's not depressing, it's just doing something that will make you look better.

But just because jeans have got so much better doesn't mean that they are fail-safe. To be honest, they've actually got trickier because there are so many possible jeans styles around, and magazines that tell you everybody should wear this style or that style, when the truth is – obviously – no one style is going to suit everyone. More than any other piece of clothing, jeans can show off your figure to its best, but if you get the wrong cut or style they will do you absolutely no favours at all.

The first thing to think about is, naturally, the money issue. I wear jeans more or less every day so it makes sense to me to spend that little bit more on something that my bottom will be relying on so much. But the high street, as it almost always does, has risen to the challenge quite commendably and you can get great jeans there. Abercrombie & Fitch's styles and denims are very good and I often pick up a couple of pieces when I go to the States. You can buy them online through www.abercrombieandfitch.com.

But if you have time and money, it's great to buy your jeans from a specific denim store or a knowledgeable boutique as the shop assistants in there will be able to help you much more and they'll be more willing to spend the necessary amount of time with you that it takes to choose. Levi's stores are good and the best place in London is probably Start on Rivington Street, which has a great selection of jeans as well as

I wear jeans more or less every day so it makes sense to me to spend that

really interesting non-denim clothes by cult and smaller designers.

One way of telling whether a jeans shop is any good is by the mirrors in the changing rooms: any denim shop with a bit of nous will have multi-way mirrors so you can get every possible view of yourself, particularly your bottom. Actually, all changing rooms should have these but getting the full perspective is especially important when it comes to denim.

Although it is definitely a good investment to buy a pair of well-cut jeans, it's

little bit more on something that my bottom will be relying on so much

surprising how few there are out there. I will not spend my money on something that doesn't make me look good, and nor should you.

A common problem is that if the jeans are tight enough around the leg they're then too tight in the waist. And speaking of the waist, the waistband shouldn't be too thick and heavy because it will dig painfully into your hips and that gives everyone the hated muffin-top look. Check that the waistband doesn't do that annoying gaping thing at the back, either, as you'll end up with a weird wind-tunnel effect. Radcliffe jeans are cut higher at the back so not only do they not gape but also they don't give you builder's bottom every time you sit down.

Jeans that bag around the knees or bottom are another fashion disaster and it's amazing how many designers don't pay attention to this, considering a major point of jeans is to make those parts of your body look good. For instance, I really like skinny-fit jeans, but some can sometimes start bagging around the knees after a couple of wears, and they flatten my bottom as opposed to acting like a Wonderbra on it, as a pair of jeans should. 7 For All Mankind jeans are also hugely popular but, personally, I find them a bit middle of the road – you know, clothes that make you look OK, but they're not exactly exciting. For me, they're not cut tight enough on the legs or low enough on the hips. Instead, I like Superfine, which has a really good skinny cut; Acne Jeans do a nice straight leg, ending at just the right point around your heels; and Moto jeans from Topshop are cute, come in great washes and, of course, very good value. But because I am, as you can see, completely obsessive about jeans, I actually designed my own line of jeans with Rock & Republic.

I always make sure my jeans have just a bit of stretch to them (but not too much that they bag), are narrow around the leg and give shape to the bottom instead of

Jeans by Victoria Beckham for Rock & Republic

Straight Leg

TopShop

Topshop black straight leg jeans are great – flattering but also a bit rock 'n' roll as long as you get them in a good straight or skinny cut

Boot-cut

Rock & Republic

Rock & Republic jeans are flattering, comfy and sexy. I design my own range for them

Skinny

Superfine

<u>Superfine's skinny styles</u> are really great, ending at just the right point around the heel of your shoe

Wide Leg

Radcliffe

<u>Radcliffe jeans</u> are cleverly cut higher at the back so not only do they not gape but they don't give you a builder's bum either

squashing it down. If you're quite curvy with hips and a bum, Miss Sixty is the label you want. Whereas if you have more of a straight up and down build, go for Habitual, Grass Los Angeles (which has a great back pocket design) or Acne Jeans.

It is crucial to make sure the jeans are long enough unless you particularly fancy looking like Charlie Chaplin paddling about. When trying them on, stand in front of the mirror on your tiptoes and then with flat feet, as you are likely to be wearing them with heels and trainers and you need to see how they look with both. With heels, the bottom of your jeans should just skim your toes, as that will give a good couple of inches of length to your legs without making you look like a child playing in her mother's dressing-up box. Obviously, if your jeans are long enough for heels, they're going to drag a bit with flats but that really doesn't matter and we've all got used to seeing raggedy hems from everyone treading on the backs of their jeans when they wear trainers.

If you can afford it, though, it's good to have one pair for heels and one for trainers, but don't make the mistake of getting your 'trainers jeans' too short. Like your 'heels jeans', they should end almost at the tip of the shoe, maybe even just graze the ground, and break almost at your toes. There is, however, a third option: Radcliffe jeans, which I mentioned earlier, have these clever little hooks at the bottom, meaning you can take up and let down your jeans according to your needs, so you could just get one pair of those and adjust them accordingly.

Ever since low-slung jeans came on the market a lot of people have thought that they should be the automatic choice, but that actually isn't so. True, low-slung is more flattering on short-waisted girls but flat-fronted, high-waisted jeans actually look really fashion-forward now – welcome to the cyclical fashion world! And if you're a bit self-conscious about the length of your legs, high-waisted jeans are great for elongating them. Superfine and Karen Walker do them very well and, you never know, they might work on you. I was a little wary about high-waisted jeans myself at first and thought they'd make me look completely out of proportion. But you know, they weren't bad at all. Admittedly, they do really squeeze you in round the waist and by the end of the day I was beginning to have mental images of my epitaph: Victoria Beckham – done in by denim. So I generally stick with my low-slungs.

As for colour, the absolute worst one for most body shapes is powder blue. Not only does it look really fifteen years ago but it is guaranteed to make your legs look twice as wide as they actually are, which, in my experience, is not generally what women want from their jeans. Whiskerings – those little crease lines that happen at the top of your jeans legs – are fine if they occur naturally, but a lot of jeans companies put them in to make the jeans look more vintage and they inevitably just end up looking really contrived.

You have to be careful with some trends, for

example those bleached-out faded patches on jeans under the bottom and on the front of thighs. In some cases you could end up looking like you've been sitting with a puppy that hasn't been house-trained on your lap.

Black jeans are great as long as you get them in a good cut, such as the ones that Superfine championed in 2004 and 2005. But remember: skinny black is rock 'n' roll, baggy black tends to be a bit roadie. White jeans are difficult for lots of people to wear and you have to be realistic with yourself. Sure, you might like how cool they look, but if they're not working on you, what's the point?

It's the same with sizing. Yes, you want a pair of jeans that is good and slim on the legs but that does not mean you should try to squeeze yourself into a pair that is just too small because you can't face the idea of going up a size. Wearing something that is obviously too small is never a good look, whatever size is on the label. Plus, it is just depressing wearing something all day that is digging into you, making you feel miserable and uncomfortable. Buy the right size and just cut out the label at home, and you'll pretty soon forget whatever that number was because you'll be too busy admiring how fantastic you look. Or you can be like my mum, who always says, 'I am a size 10 but a size 12 is so much more comfortable!'

The ideal pair of jeans is flattering, comfy and sexy and that tends to mean blue, slim and boot-cut. There was a lot of excitement in the past year about skinny jeans and, yes, they can look cool. But boot-cut jeans are more versatile. You can wear them with heels and flats; but if I were to wear flats with skinny jeans I'd look like a golf club. Yes, Kate Moss can get away with the skinny jeans and flats look, but that's because she's Kate Moss! Just because something looks good on someone else does not mean it will look good on you. This rule is doubly true for anything she wears because, sadly, very few of us look like her.

One exception to the Kate rule, though, is tucking jeans into boots. As far as I can tell, she made this fashionable again and it is the most fantastically useful look as it is not only so easy, and looks a bit cooler than just boots under jeans, but also it keeps your jeans dry and clean on rainy days – a crucial consideration if jeans are part of your almost daily wardrobe and you live in Britain. Couple of things to remember: first, make sure the jeans are tucked in nice and snug and don't, as often happens, bag around the knee, or you will look like you're playing Billy Bunter in some Christmas

The ideal pair of jeans is flattering, comfy and sexy and that tends to mean blue, slim and boot-cut

panto. I have to admit, skinny jeans are best for this as then you won't look like you've got some weird growth inside your boots around your ankles, which can happen with boot-cut because there is much more excess fabric swishing about at the ankles.

But if you don't have any skinny jeans, you can tuck the ends of your fitted bootleg jeans into tight long socks. This can squeeze your legs a bit so maybe it's the perfect outfit to wear on long-haul flights to ward off deep-vein thrombosis! And you thought I was just here for fashion tips . . .

As for the boots, they should end right below your knee and not, as too many boots do, midway up your calf, since this cuts off your leg at the widest point. Skinny jeans tucked into an ankle boot is more of a fashion thing than a style thing, by which I mean it isn't a classic look, but one that only looks good if it's currently going through a moment.

I wear denim almost every day and as a general guideline I'd recommend one pair of boot-cut and one pair of skinny

As for how many pairs of jeans you should own, well, it obviously depends on how often you wear them. As you can tell, I wear denim almost every day so I have quite a few pairs and I try to get them in as many different styles as possible. But as a general guideline I'd recommend one pair of boot-cut and one pair of skinny. If you can stretch to a few more, get a pair that slip very flatteringly around the hip and are loose in the legs – boyfriend style, as they're called, because they look like you borrowed them from your boyfriend; these look really cute with trainers.

The absolute worst thing anyone can do with their jeans – worse than tapered legs, powder blue and too-tight waistbands combined – is to pull their G-string over the waistband. There was a period a few years ago when it seemed that everybody and their dog was being photographed falling out of Chinawhite with their G-string hoiked above their jeans. I don't mind a bit of lingerie showing, like a pretty bra strap under a vest top, or maybe even a peek underneath a dress or shirt, like Dolce & Gabbana have been doing since the label first started back in the 80s. But that is very different from bending over in Piccadilly Circus and showing your thong.

It's the same with wearing your jeans super-low slung. A few years back there seemed to be a competition about who could wear the lowest slung jeans, showing off as much crotch as possible. Not only is it unattractive but it must be extremely uncomfortable as surely you'd constantly feel like your jeans were falling down. Plus, you'd have to work extra hard to find a T-shirt long enough to meet the waistband of your jeans because that whole belly-flashing thing is totally passé now.

Moving on from denim, trousers in general are tricky to buy because you are so dependent on the cut. Generally speaking, you want a slim pair that skims your figure, is loose at the ankle (in other words, NOT tapered), in a good, heavyish fabric like a wool/cotton mix. This will fall better and be less likely to give you VPL – something you should always, ALWAYS check for before leaving the house. As with

AS WITH JEANS, BOOT-CUT TROUSERS GENERALLY TEND TO BE THE MOST FLATTERING AND VERSATILE, SO THEY ARE MY USUAL CHOICE

jeans, you can go high-waisted or low-waisted, depending on which part of your body you feel more confident about emphasizing – the hips or the waist – and the proportion of your legs to your torso. And, again, as with jeans, boot-cut trousers generally tend to be the most flattering and versatile, so they are my usual choice, although I do have a very flared pair which I really love as they make me feel very 70s David Bowie, in a rather fabulous sort of way. But wearing them is definitely a look, meaning I then have to think about what I wear them with and where to, as opposed to something I can just throw on.

For that, the trousers I wear most frequently are black and boot-cut. I know people complain that women wear black trousers too often but I don't really see the problem since they make so many people look so good. Wearing a totally black outfit can be sexy in an understated way and make you feel confident, as you know everything goes. For example, the other day when I went out for lunch I wore some black cord trousers, a black polo neck and big black sunglasses. But this works only if you don't begin to rely on black too much, like a crutch. Then you will start to feel a bit dreary and that will reflect in how you look.

As with jeans, make sure that the trousers have good length in the leg for your high heels and that they give your bottom a bit of a lift instead of flattening it or just bagging around it shapelessly.

But trousers have one potential problem that most jeans don't, and I think if I say you need to make sure the trousers are not too tight in the front of the crotch, you'll know what I mean. You don't want to give people more than an eyeful in that area. I'm always amazed how many women seem to leave the house without checking for this very obvious and highly embarrassing issue. The trick is simply to buy trousers that are flat-fronted and sufficiently roomy in the crotch, even going a size up, if necessary, and then getting them taken in around the waist and legs by a good dry-cleaner or tailor.

The ultimate trousers are by Balenciaga, a label that has always specialized in an almost couture level of cutting. Even though the original Christobal Balenciaga died over thirty years ago, the brand, led by Creative Director Nicolas Ghesquière, still makes some of the most perfect – and, unsurprisingly, most expensive – trousers and jackets in the world.

Stella McCartney and Dolce & Gabbana also make fantastic trousers, but these too require some serious cash. However they do last for years so once you buy a pair, that's it. The high street do some great trousers too, particularly at Reiss and Topshop.

Always check when you're buying trousers that they really are working for your figure. In other words, if you're not a pear, there's no need to buy pear-shaped trousers. Square peg, round hole, to put it simply.

I love corduroy trousers as they have that casual – but sexy – look of jeans, but are a little more original, with a 70s kick to them too. This is particularly true of ones with that very 70s Farrah cut to them – flat-fronted with a narrow then lightly flared leg. Joe's Jeans does a good denim version and most corduroy trousers today take a similar inspiration. All the rules for jeans (check the cut, check your every view) and trousers (check the crotch area) apply to cords, and make sure you always get the thin-ribbed cords. Not only do wide ribs actually make your legs look bigger, they also look so outdated and remind me of the kind of thing my mum used to wear to the Starlight Rooms in the 80s. Cool then, maybe, definitely not now. Incidentally, the rule about thin ribs applies to all ribbed clothing, from vest tops to wool tights, for exactly the same reasons as corduroy. The best thin-ribbed vests, in my experience, come from American labels such as Abercrombie & Fitch (one of my favourite brands) and James Perse, but, equally, you can often get good ones from

Petit Bateau. Going back to corduroy trousers, Rock & Republic do very good ones and you can get some cute pairs on the high street these days. But if you really love them, stock up when you're in America or France as they are more popular there and are therefore more widely available.

Combat trousers can work if you're going for the urban look, but make sure you get ones that suit your body type. The best – and often the cheapest – come from army surplus stores, such as Laurence Corner and Jungle, as they are authentic and less gimmicky than the ones you find on the high street. Be careful, though, that you give your vintage combats a wash before wearing them because, no matter how good your trousers look, smelling like a sweaty soldier won't help your image at all.

I really love cropped trousers and they can be worn in almost every season. But whatever material you get yours in – denim, tweed, cotton or wool – and whether you're going for a formal or casual look, make sure they end about three-quarters of the way down your calf, just at the point where it starts to narrow towards your ankle. This is the most flattering cut-off point on your leg: any higher and it ends at the widest part of your calf and your legs will look like sausages, any lower and it will just look like you shrunk your trousers in the wash. As for what shoes to wear with cut-off trousers, this is where a lot of women make mistakes and think, well, last time cut-offs were in I wore white stilettos so I'll wear white stilettos again. When something from your past comes back into fashion – cut-off trousers, flared trousers or long skirts – this does not mean you should wear them exactly as you did ten years ago. Secondly, the whole point of certain looks coming back into fashion is to show us how we can do it differently this time round, usually even better. So last summer, for example, I wore my cut-offs with a pair of chunky-heeled round-toed shoes, which looked far more current than a pair of white stilettos! Always watch out that you don't get stuck in a fashion time warp: it's very easy to be complacent and to dress exactly the same as you've been doing for the past however many years, but not only will that look probably not suit you any more, you'll look hopelessly out of date. And as you can see, you needn't be scared about updating your look as it really isn't difficult: it's just a matter of doing

Shoe by Topshop Vintage

Last summer, I wore my cut-offs with a pair of chunky-heeled round-toed shoes, which looked far more current than a pair of white stilettos something as simple as switching from pointed-toe shoes to round toes, or from stilettos to chunky heels. This is not a matter of blindly following trends that don't suit you, but rather it's about keeping an eye on making sure you don't fall into a style rut.

With cut-off trousers, I recommend wearing high heels. However, flats with slim, cigarette trousers (in other words, not gripping the leg but closely fitting around it) is very Audrey Hepburn in *Funny Face*, or Jean Seberg in *A Bout de Souffle* – two very good looks to go for. Flip-flops with cropped trousers are, of course, a summer staple.

As cropped trousers are quite a French look, I have found that French companies, like Agnès B, do them best. But plenty of British high-street stores now do cut-off jeans really well, in both narrow and wide leg.

Boots under cut-off trousers are OK as long as the top of the boot is completely under the hem of the trousers. To have a gap of skin between the boot and the trousers is the leg's equivalent of that belly flashing when your top is too short to meet the top of your jeans: it's unflattering, very unsexy and totally truncates your body. In fact, make sure the boot is a good couple of inches under your trouser hem so that you don't get that gap, even when you sit down and cross your legs.

Shorts have made a comeback and, as I live in a pretty hot country these days, I'm so pleased about this. I recommend the Topshop and Chloe versions which end just above the knee, with a flat front, zippered or buttoned fly (DEFINITELY not an elasticated waist on knee-lengths as the fabric will then bunch out and billow around the hips) and a loose but body-following cut. They can be worn with a little heel or delicate flats – never trainers, unless you're off for a round of golf. When I wear shorts in the summer, I tend to pair them with a simple T-shirt and thick-heeled boots to make the look a bit more grown-up instead of looking too cutesy cute. Home-made cut-off denim shorts are always useful and you can totally control how you want them to look as you're the one making them! But longer, neater versions are also available, such as straight knee-length ones from Superfine and Serfontaine, and the high street has started to do similar ones that are basically what they call 'city shorts' in denim. Moto ones from Topshop are very well cut, sitting nicely on

Make sure the trousers are not too tight in the front of the crotch, you'll

know what I mean. You don't want to give people more than an eyeful

Cut-off denim shorts are always useful and you can totally control how you want them to look

the hip. But, in general, I think this can be a pretty hard look to pull off – they don't have the simplicity of jeans or the cuteness of shorts, and they put the emphasis on your knees in a way normal shorts just don't.

I do understand that a lot of women might be a bit nervous about wearing super-short shorts and denim 'city shorts' might seem the more wearable alternative, but, really, I think for most people your basic, looser and slightly longer shorts will look more flattering.

WHERE TO SHOP

1. BOYISH JEANS *Gap, Moto at Topshop, Lee*

2. STRAIGHT JEANS *Habitual, Rock & Republic, H&M, Abercrombie & Fitch, Grass Los Angeles, Acne Jeans, Levi's, Pepe, Wrangler*

3. CURVY JEANS *Miss Sixty, Radcliffe*

4. SKINNY JEANS *Superfine, Moto at Topshop, Sass & Bide*

5. HIGH-WAISTED JEANS

Karen Walker, Superfine, Joe's Jeans

6. LOW-WAISTED JEANS *Tsubi, Frankie B*

7. DESIGNER TROUSERS

Stella McCartney, Balenciaga, Dolce & Gabbana, Chloe, Burberry Prorsum, Vanessa Bruno, Marc by Marc Jacobs

8. HIGH-STREET TROUSERS

Reiss, Zara, French Connection, Agnès B

9. CORDUROY TROUSERS

Rock & Republic, 7 For All Mankind, Topshop

10. CROPPED TROUSERS & JEANS

Agnès B, Fornarina, Gap, Rock & Republic

11. SHORTS *Chloe, Topshop, Gap*

Jeans

39

Tops

Cotton blouse by SEE BY CHLOE;
Cotton T-shirt by A.P.C.; Cotton
vest by ABERCROMBIE & FITCH

WHEN YOU'RE GETTING DRESSED FIRST THING IN THE MORNING, THE TRICK IS NOT TO PULL OUT JUST ANY OLD GARMENTS

AND PILE THEM ON WITHOUT THINKING ABOUT IT, BUT TO VISUALIZE THE WHOLE OUTFIT BEFORE YOU START – think about the end product, if you like, figuring out what bag would go with the dress, what you should then do with your hair, and so on, so you know the look you're going for from the start. Gordon Ramsay told me he does the same thing when cooking, visualizing the whole meal in advance and then pulling the ingredients together. Funnily enough, David said he applies the same thing to football, so perhaps it's a lesson you can apply to all walks of life!

It's often with tops that it all starts to go wrong. You may decide to wear something because it's on the top of the pile in your drawer, or because it will keep you warm enough, or just because it will do and you're in a hurry, whether or not it goes with the rest of your outfit. As a mother of three, I'm always rushing around in the mornings and don't have much time to fiddle about in my wardrobe so I often work out my outfit the night before, thinking which tops would go with which trousers or skirts. For example, recently I wore a long multicoloured skirt I bought from a vintage shop, a Zara vest and an Alexander McQueen bolero – in other words, clothes from very different ends of the fashion spectrum, but I felt they worked together. It's through mixing and matching, but careful planning, that you make the outfit your own. Then you can experiment and do things like putting a corset on top of your blouse or, for a more casual version of the look, vests on top of T-shirts.

Any cut that plunges is going to make your neck look longer, whereas one that ends right under your throat can truncate it and can be less sexy

I'd suggest you buy your vests and T-shirts from the high street. C&C California, which is based in California, pretty much started off the trend for simple shirts and their versions are still fantastic, with a long smooth cut and extra-long sleeves. Even when you've bunged them in the washing machine 100 times they keep their softness and shape. They are, though, a little more expensive. Stock up on them if you go to the States as they're much cheaper there. The American west coast generally makes the best T-shirts, with companies like James Perse also based there. It's for the same reason that so many of the best jeans labels come from the west: California specializes in that laid-back but pulled-together look. So it's not surprising they do the informal basics so well.

But the high street has really picked up on this recently, particularly Gap, H&M and Mango, so you don't need to look across the Atlantic for a decent T-shirt. In terms of cuts, scoop necks and V-necks look lovely on most women as they elongate the neck. Obviously, any cut that plunges is going to make your neck look longer whereas one that ends right under your throat can truncate it and can be less sexy. I stock up on T-shirts and V-necks at Topshop all the time.

You see increasing numbers of square-necked tops these days. These are also great because they're more unusual than scoop necks and V-necks but they operate in the same way to lengthen your neck. Basically, just letting your collarbones show is very sexy – actually, almost more sexy than showing off your cleavage because you give a hint of bareness without being clichéd and obvious. Because square-necked tops look a bit more formal than V-necks and scoop necks, they go best with a more formal outfit, such as smart trousers or a pencil skirt, both of which balance out the broadening effect of the square neck on top as they are narrower on your bottom half. Scoop necks, on the other hand, are very casual and can be worn just with a simple denim mini or denim cut-offs; V-necks look great with jeans.

T-shirts by Topshop, Petit Bateau and Worn By

With vests, it's often a good idea to get them a size bigger than you need just to make sure that they're long enough, and it doesn't matter so much if they're a bit loose on the sides as you can layer them to keep your modesty intact. My favourite cut is thin-ribbed, long and with a sports back, which is much more flattering than the conventional cut as it gives a nice shape to your shoulders and back. Some vests even have built-in support for your boobs so you don't have to worry about getting a bra that won't show through your vest, a look that can be hard to carry off.

Lots of people think that wearing a bra that is the same colour as their top will stop it showing through, but this just isn't true. The material of the top will be thinner than that of your bra, so two quite noticeable triangles will be staring everyone in the face every time they look at you. You see this so often with white T-shirts in particular. Instead, wear a flesh-coloured bra underneath because what you really should be trying to match is your skin colour. That will look far more natural. The exception to this rule is if you are obviously letting your bra show through deliberately, such as when you're wearing a pretty one in a bright colour for a Dolce & Gabbana, early Madonna look. Alternatively, you can layer your vest tops, which was a big trend in 2006.

The British high street is making great vests these days – long, comfortable, flattering, in cool colours and without too much stretchy fabric in them, which always seems to have the miraculous ability of making the vest cling to your body in precisely the places you'd rather it didn't. Length, too, is key as this will give you a much nicer shape and will make you look far more pulled together than having a flash of skin poking out. The classic colours I recommend for T-shirts and vests are plain navy blue, black, slate grey and white – the most useful colours when it comes to tops as they go with almost everything. Once you find a T-shirt and vest make that you like, buy as many as you can afford because a well-fitting T-shirt is a precious find and stores have an evil habit of discontinuing your perfect style soon after you find it. But just because you might bulk-buy the same style, make sure you get it in

top will stop it showing through, but this just isn't true ...

different shades. It's very easy to keep buying the same thing that you already have – after all, you loved it enough to buy it originally so inevitably and instinctively you'll keep being drawn back to it. But this isn't necessary because, well, you already have it! This is true not just for vest colours but for everything in your wardrobe, from shoe styles to skirt lengths. Make sure you always go for variations, even if it is on the same theme, otherwise you'll find you have nothing to wear for certain occasions and you'll just make yourself sick of the look after wearing it so much. I'm not a fan of cropped T-shirts. A simple T-shirt, a vintage belt and a good pair of jeans is a much cooler look. Cap sleeves are particularly popular with high-street stores but they can be tricky. Often they are cut so narrowly they practically cut off

I'm not a massive fan of cropped T-shirts. A simple T-shirt, a vintage belt and a good pair of jeans is a much cooler look

your blood supply, which looks as unflattering and uncomfortable as a waistband that's too tight. They also rub into your armpit badly, meaning you'll probably get massive sweat patches; most definitely not a good look either.

Little puffed shoulders on T-shirts have become popular recently and they do help to make your top look more feminine as well as flattering your upper arm. On the high street three-quarter-length sleeves seem to be everywhere. And there is something quite seductive about them as they give an unexpected flash of skin. Back in the eighteenth and early nineteenth centuries, just catching a glimpse of a woman's ankle was seen as outrageously sexy. The trick still works: showing just a tiny bit of flesh, subtly, as opposed to getting it all out, makes the look more tantalizing. But because of this ladylike appeal, three-quarter sleeves look best worn with modest or more grown-up pieces, such as smart trousers or a pencil skirt. After all, if you wear a three-quarter-sleeve top with a miniskirt, you totally ruin the impact of showing your wrist. It might sound weird, I know, but, honestly, it works.

With long-sleeved shirts, make sure the sleeves are actually long enough, i.e. not ending halfway down your wrist, otherwise your top will look like it's shrunk in the wash. If you're wearing a T-shirt, wear a smooth T-shirt bra beneath it, not a frilly lace one as the lace will poke through the T-shirt and make it look as though you have bumpy breasts. So just go for a plain, underwired, T-shirt bra, such as one from Calvin Klein Underwear. Lastly, don't wear a push-up bra under a tight T-shirt as that really is too obvious. What you should be aiming for is a nice simple line, not trying to hoik your boobs up your nostrils.

Cardigan

I really like cardigans and, worn
correctly, they can be really sexy.
They either have to be super slim
or really long and chunky –
anything in between just looks
dull and frumpy. I love wearing
the really thick and long ones,
either from TOPSHOP, JOSEPH
or by STELLA McCARTNEY:
you can really snuggle on down
in them, and maybe even belt
them up

Vest

My favourite make is
ABERCROMBIE & FITCH,
which is an American label, and
their vests are really fantastic –
thin-ribbed, long and with a
sports back – which is much more
flattering than the conventional
cut as it gives a nice shape to
your shoulders and back

V-Neck

In the winter I rely on polo necks and cashmere V-necks and I almost always get these from the high street, particularly GAP and TOPSHOP. I think a V-neck jumper, scarf and jeans is a perfect winter date outfit

Blouse

Blouses have come back in thanks in a large part to CHLOE, who have been making some beautiful blouses. The best way to wear them is just with a pair of jeans, a vintage belt and boots

Patterned T-shirts are OK – I've got some really pretty vintage ones – but I do find plain ones more useful. Big prints can look good but I think it's best just to limit them to your accessories because they can be a little gimmicky on clothes and it's really noticeable if you wear them too often. In my opinion, patterns can be more challenging and are the equivalent of someone jumping up and down and shouting, 'Look at my outfit! Hey! Over here! Check it out!' Plain colours, however, are subtler and you can recycle them as much as you like and no one ever notices. They're easier to layer and just go with more of the clothes in your wardrobe. And because patterns are so distinctive, they can pick up certain associations: look what happened to Burberry just a few years ago when its house check pattern turned up everywhere. Burberry's Creative Director, Christopher Bailey, and his creative team, began to focus instead on emphasizing the brand's heritage and reputation for quality rather than over-exposing the checks, and using them in a more subtle, modern way. But it was a good lesson in how a famous pattern can slip all too easily into just being infamous.

Also, be wary of tops with horizontal stripes. One of my mother's style rules when I was a child was never to wear horizontal stripes, and that has always stayed with me. My mum's other style tip, incidentally, is don't eat beetroot because it stains, and I never have to this day.

Some T-shirts with slogans are OK – some are even fashion classics. Katharine Hamnett's T-shirts from the 80s, with oversized political statements, remain one of the defining looks from that decade, and it's impossible to talk about 70s fashion without mentioning the Sex Pistols' T-shirts and Vivienne Westwood's punk pieces, and the impact they had on popularizing the punk movement. The sloganned T-shirts that are the worst are the ones that are plastered all over with a designer's name, though I have occasionally, in the past, been a culprit myself. These are what I call designer-designer clothes – clothes that just draw attention to the fact that they're made by a designer by being covered either in logos or with someone's name. If the clothes are good, they'll speak for themselves.

Sloganned clothes I will make an exception for are vintage rock 'n' roll T-shirts.

The classic colours I recommend for T-shirts and vests are ... navy blue,

black, slate grey and white — the most useful colours when it comes to tops

Clutch by Fendi

Shrunken Michael Jackson's *Bad* tour T-shirts? Madonna 'Material Girl' pieces? How can anyone not enjoy those? Wear them with good jeans and heels and you look cool, casual and show you have a sense of humour, which is always attractive. You can always find these in any half-decent second-hand vintage shop and, unless they're really rare, they are dead cheap. Urban Outfitters does them too, and you can find mocked-up ones all over the high street – H&M do good ones. On a trip to New York recently, I went to one of my favourite vintage shops, What Goes Around Comes Around, and picked up for David T-shirts from tours by the Beatles, U2 and Abba, which looked just fantastic on him. But no, David is not a secret Abba fan, so let's stop that rumour now.

A word about vintage, though: it's easy to get confused about the difference between vintage and second-hand and that's because they're basically the same. But when I say vintage, I mean something that is relatively old, looks unique and has been checked by an expert to make sure it's good quality. You don't necessarily have to go to a specialist vintage store to get good pieces since you can find them in second-hand charity shops, like Oxfam. Actually, I've given away some pieces to charity shops myself, so you never know, you might walk out with something from my wardrobe for a fiver! In vintage shops, though, they'll generally know more about the history of the clothes and the pieces will have been chosen because there's something special about them, as opposed to being stocked just because people donated them.

A good-fitting T-shirt always looks pulled together, even just a pair of good shoes, a great bag and sunglasses will do the trick

LK Bennett

French Connection

BLOUSES HAVE COME BACK IN RECENTLY, THANKS IN A
LARGE PART TO CHLOE'S FORMER CREATIVE DIRECTOR,
PHOEBE PHILO, who sadly left the company. During her time at Chloe, she
showed how a blouse doesn't have to make you look like a Sunday School marm but
can actually be very youthful, very cool and very, if subtly, sexy. The best way to
wear them is just with a pair of jeans, a vintage-looking belt and boots; with a
miniskirt they can look a bit finicky and overly girlish whereas jeans balance out the
blouse's overtly feminine style. If your blouse is relatively flouncy, with a frilled neck
– although you shouldn't go too frilly, especially if you're busty – keep your hair off
your neck otherwise you'll look like you're drowning and it all gets a bit Krystal
Carrington. The high street has done this blouse thing really well, with very pretty,
well-made ones that have taken clever cues from designers, particularly, of course,
Chloe. Cult designers such as 3.1 Phillip Lim have also made beautiful blouses, and

Sara Berman   Chloe

even what look like blouses lengthened into dresses. Just make sure your blouse is not too see-through and, if it is, slip on a white vest or something similarly simple underneath, but check that the vest is as long as the blouse or you'll have that inch or two of tummy visible through your blouse, which can look a bit fussy no matter how good your tummy is, or how ladylike your blouse.

For long-sleeved blouses, the best sleeve style is slightly billowing and then cinched in at the cuff as this gives your arm a willowy, elegant appearance. It's one of those looks that girls love and boys just wonder why we're trying to look like milkmaids.

An easy way to make your blouse stand out a little more is to replace the plastic buttons that blouses often have with some pretty vintage buttons, or just unusual-looking ones. There are lots of great button shops in London, such as The Button Queen in Marylebone and The Button Shop in east London, but equally you can just go to somewhere like John Lewis or the button stalls in Portobello and Camden markets. This is a handy tip for all items of clothing, by the way, particularly coats, and can individualize a basic high-street piece to make it look much more striking.

To be honest, I usually find blouses a little too frilly for my taste and instead I prefer to go for men's white shirts cut for women. I really love this look because it's

Waistcoats have always been a great way to sex up a pair of jeans . . . just swapping the pretty top for a waistcoat with nothing underneath looks more modern

sexy but clean and sharp. Dolce & Gabbana pretty much coined this sexy masculine look back in the 80s and showed how it can be very alluring, for example with a few buttons undone and a good pencil skirt or pair of trousers, and the look, impressively, has never dated. Just make sure the shirt is crisp, well tailored, fitting all the way up to under your arms and with a good, starchy collar. Gucci and Dolce & Gabbana are the masters of this look but Thomas Pink also do them. Shirts cut for women can still sometimes hang in a bit of a shapeless way, so nip them in with a wide belt that sits right above your trousers or skirt, almost like a cummerbund, to give them a feminine shape. Then just wear the shirt either tucked in or over your waistband.

Speaking of men's clothes, waistcoats have always been a great way to sex up a pair of jeans. I have bought a lot of vintage men's waistcoats from second-hand stores and had them taken in at the back to fit. The high street has picked up on them in a big way, making sharp ones specifically for women so you don't even need to bother with altering them.

Whilst I'm not a fan myself, a halterneck top is another alternative to wear with your jeans on a night out and some are very pretty, particularly ones from high-street stores like Paul & Joe and Whistles. Make sure you wear a bra with them (Marks & Spencer and La Senza do good halterneck ones) as if you don't, and if it's a bit chilly that night, well, everyone will be able to tell just by looking at your top. After all, you don't want to look like you could tune yourself into Radio 1!

I hate feeling cold, like a lot of women, but bundling up under loads of layers isn't my style. Instead, in the winter I rely on polo necks and cashmere V-neck jumpers and I almost always buy these from the high street, particularly Topshop, whose jumpers are often cut just brilliantly. That's what I mean about buying the simple basics from the high street and maybe spending a little more on things like trousers

The great thing about cute cardigans is they give you layering and

where the cut really does matter. Just remember, if you do wear a polo neck, to keep your hair simple and your neck as clear as possible. It's best not to wear a necklace over one, as I did the day after David and I got engaged – honestly, I look at those photos and can't imagine what I was thinking, although David, bless him, still insists he thinks I looked lovely. Anyway, you never know, what with fashion being such a cyclical game and all, maybe necklaces and polo necks will be all over the catwalks next season . . . ! But, personally, I think keeping things as clean as possible is what generally works best. Polo necks, like all jumpers, should be either super-fitted or deliberately thick and baggy; everything in between just looks sloppy.

A V-neck jumper, scarf and jeans make a perfect winter-date outfit, and I really love cashmere or fine-wool jumper dresses, which we'll talk about later.

Jumpers can be tricky: if you get a well-cut, well-knit one, you look fabulous; anything less just looks frumpy. Toast has some nice slim-knit and beautifully coloured ones, as does Brora, although those are certainly pricier. Pure make the most incredibly soft cashmere and Alex Gore Brown is probably the best young knitwear designer around her stuff is so much sexier than you'd think knitwear could possibly be. Sticking at this mid- to high-end price range, Sara Berman makes really cute and very original-looking jumpers and full, well-fitting knitted dresses. Marc by Marc Jacobs does sweet and kitschily patterned jumpers every winter, and Bella Freud makes gorgeous ones that are super-thin and very well fitted, perfect for layering under short-sleeved dresses. Sonia Rykiel is also good on knits, particularly long knitted dresses, and hers often have a tongue-in-cheek humour to them. If you really want to blow the budget, probably the best designer knitwear comes from Missoni, Chanel and Pringle. Chanel first made knitted sweaters fashionable in the 20s, and then Pringle went onto create the cardigan twinset in the 30s (they celebrated the twinset's seventieth anniversary in 2004). A Chanel cardigan is extremely expensive – we're talking in the neighbourhood of £1,000 here – but keep an eye out for them in charity shops and vintage stores as you never know what people might give away. It might surprise some people but Julien Macdonald actually started out in knitwear, making very intricate woollen jumpers and dresses. But he's best known now, of

warmth but still show off the shape of your body instead of hiding it course, for fabulous dresses.

Cardigans have had a lot of bad press in the past but, worn correctly, they can be very stylish. I love wearing the really thick and long ones, either from Topshop or by Stella McCartney or Balenciaga: you can snuggle down in them, and maybe even belt them up and wear them like a dress with some high-heeled boots. The very cropped cardigans, which end halfway up your back and are almost boleros, look great and are far sexier than a baggy old V-neck jumper. They look a bit *Flashdance* in a good way. The great thing about them is that they give you layering and warmth but still show off the shape of your body instead of hiding it beneath huge swathes of material. Embellished cropped cardigans have become very popular, and it's not surprising as they are just so useful. They can totally make an outfit, even if you are wearing just jeans and a vest, and are perfect to wear with a strappy party dress for a night out. Marc by Marc Jacobs and Day Birger et Mikkelsen make very beautiful ones and you can find similarly pretty ones on the high street.

Boleros can be a little harder to find on the high street. It's generally easier to hunt them down in vintage outlets like Beyond Retro in east London. You can occasionally find them in designers' diffusion ranges, like Marc by Marc Jacobs and Sonia by Sonia Rykiel. If you want a designer one, Alexander McQueen does them beautifully.

Sweatshirts and hooded tops can look quite cute and sporty, as long as you get well-fitting, almost shrunken ones. American Apparel fit beautifully. Marc by Marc Jacobs also does sweet little hooded tops, often in kitschy prints.

One outfit people often ask me about is the tracksuit, and my response is always the same: for non-photographic occasions only. They're great for slobbing around the house in on Sunday mornings and for long-haul flights, but it is hard to find ones that look good, so everyone ends up wearing the same one label. Generally, I am more of a jeans person anyway, but I do love Juicy tracksuits – they are cosy, come in such great colours and have the sexiest cut. So I do wear them while hanging out at home with David and the kids. But you can't have another footballer's wife out and about being photographed in a Juicy Couture tracksuit!

WHERE TO SHOP

1. T-SHIRTS *Polo Ralph Lauren, Abercrombie & Fitch, Topshop, H&M, Gap, Mango, C&C California, American Apparel, Velvet, Ella Moss*

2. LONG-SLEEVED T-SHIRTS *C&C California, American Apparel*

3. BOLEROS *Beyond Retro, Topshop, Marc by Marc Jacobs, Sonia by Sonia Rykiel*

4. VESTS *Abercrombie & Fitch, James Perse, Vince, Topshop, Zara, Mango, C&C California, Petit Bateau*

5. BLOUSES *Chloe, 3.1 Phillip Lim, Whistles, H&M, Topshop, Paul & Joe*

6. MEN'S-STYLE SHIRTS *Gucci, Dolce & Gabbana, Thomas Pink, Margaret Howell, Paul Smith, Gap, school-uniform departments*

7. WAISTCOATS *Topshop, H&M, Beyond Retro, Sonia by Sonia Rykiel*

8. V-NECK TOPS *Topshop, H&M*

9. HALTERNECKS *Paul & Joe, Whistles*

10. CARDIGANS *Chanel, Balenciaga, Marc by Marc Jacobs, Joseph, Day Birger et Mikkelsen, Topshop, Principles, Zara*

11. JUMPERS *Chanel, Pringle, Marc by Marc Jacobs, Missoni, Stella McCartney, Sara Berman, Bella Freud, Alex Gore Brown, Brora, Toast, Whistles, Pure, Topshop*

12. SHRUGS *Topshop, Kookai, Sonia by Sonia Rykiel, Urban Outfitters*

13. SWEATSHIRTS AND HOODED TOPS *Abercrombie & Fitch, American Apparel, Juicy Couture, Marc by Marc Jacobs, Adidas*

Skirts
& Day Dresses

Vintage prom dress from a selection at RADIO DAYS

THE QUESTION OF WHETHER TO WEAR A MINISKIRT OR A LONGER SKIRT TENDS TO SETTLE ITSELF AS YOU GET OLDER.

I USED TO WEAR MINISKIRTS ALL THE TIME IN MY TEENS AND TWENTIES, but these days, as much as I still like them, I increasingly find myself leaning more to A-line and pencil skirts that end just on or below the knee. They're elegant, but still sexy. A-line skirts are often much more flattering in proportion to your leg than miniskirts and you can wear them with some really fabulous shoes or boots. Pair an A-line skirt with a V-neck top or a cardigan and you've got a really pretty outfit that you'll feel comfortable in. You can wear it with flats for a ballerina-type look but I prefer heels to give myself a bit of a lift. Prada are known for their A-line pieces, which come in really gorgeous materials too, and Alaïa make the most perfectly cut ones in the world. For a more girly look, almost every season Cacharel and Day Birger et Mikkelsen do some sweet ones with striking patterns or embellishment. On a more realistic level, H&M can usually be relied on, and the same with Urban Outfitters. Be careful when you wear them with shoes with ankle straps as this will interrupt the relatively short leg line you already get with a knee-length skirt, making your legs look stumpy. Also, look for skirts that hug neatly around the hips before flaring out in an A-line, as opposed to falling into pleats from the hips, since the latter can give you an unfortunate tent shape. But you can have fun with patterns, if you're a fan of those, because the skirt isn't body hugging and therefore you won't look like you've been mummified in a test pattern.

One style that I really love is not exactly an A-line skirt but has a similar shape – a

One style that I really love is not exactly an A-line skirt but has a similar

starchy tulle skirt. They can really prettify an outfit in a *Sex and the City* manner and, like A-line skirts, are very flattering on the legs. You can always find them in vintage shops such as Patricia Field's shop in New York, or places like Rokit, and even Topshop, and they are almost always very cheap. Wear a narrow, body-skimming top, maybe even a plain leotard, to balance out the volume on your bottom half. And don't forget: you can always wear your tulle skirt underneath a plainer one, acting like an old-fashioned hoop skirt.

Of course, I'm not dismissing miniskirts. Anyone who has ever seen photos of Naomi Campbell, Cindy Crawford, Christy Turlington and Linda Evangelista working the miniskirt look on the Versace catwalk back in the 80s knows that they can look undeniably fantastic. I still love to wear them in the summer. Dolce & Gabbana and Roberto Cavalli make fabulous ones, Luella and PPQ make cool, sporty ones and there are endless options on the high street. You just need to bear in mind how to balance the look. For example, if you're wearing quite a little miniskirt, counteract it with a modest cardigan over a non-cleavage-tastic top, tone down your make-up and keep your hair simple. And make sure that the skirt is not so short that everyone can see your knickers whenever you bend over or get out of a car. For that matter, make sure you're wearing knickers – which may seem like an obvious point but I've seen people getting out of cars with no knickers on! Whatever people say about my clothes, and God knows people have said a lot, I've always dressed for myself in a way that makes me feel comfortable – and that does not mean wearing a miniskirt with no knickers!

Occasionally, you can find miniskirts with built-in knickers to really protect your modesty, which I think is a genius idea. Failing that, it's Bridget Jones-style knickers underneath! But seriously, boyshorts, in this instance, are generally a safer bet than a G-string. Be careful

shape – a starchy tulle skirt. They can really prettify an outfit

when wearing denim skirts as they have an unfortunate habit of slipping upwards all too easily whenever you sit down. A little too 'ride 'em cowboy', if you know what I mean.

Denim skirts are also prone to sagging a little at the front of your waistband after too many wears, giving you a funny bulge around the tummy, or making it look like your skirt is straining to hold in a pot belly. The best way to avoid this is just to look after them properly: wash them frequently at a cool temperature and lay them out flat to dry.

Also, always check your back view before you buy any kind of miniskirt. So often you see people in the street wearing minis that are just WAY too short at the back. I've also noticed some miniskirts that designers have rather cleverly just cut longer in the back.

Long skirts can look elegant but wear them with a structured or even quite sexy top to balance out the proportions – definitely not a peasant top, as that was done to death in 2005. Now, there's a good example of how a trend can really kill a look. Keep your top half clean and uncluttered: wear just a vest, for example, and, instead of a cardigan, go for a bolero or even a shrug so you don't have anything loose around your torso at all.

Of course, you can reverse the proportions and wear a plain short skirt and then a really ruffly top, but if you have a bust and long hair this can make you end up looking strangely top-heavy and a bit stifled.

However you're built, be mindful of the rule that if you get your boobs out, put your legs away and vice-versa. I guarantee you will look better and feel a lot more confident and comfortable, which will then really come across in your whole attitude. Yeah, miniskirts can be sexy but spending the whole evening tugging the wretched thing down because you feel too exposed is definitely not.

The puffball skirt has made a comeback. But to be honest, I think there's a possibility that you'd look back in a year's time and ask, seriously, 'What was I thinking?' just as we do when we look back at its 80s incarnation. The puffball has what I think is called a Challenging Shape. I'm not really into this challenging-shape concept – why wear something that is more than likely going to make you look all out of proportion? 'Challenging' seems to me to be just another word for 'unflattering'. Who wants to be challenged by their outfit, anyway? Life can be hard enough without getting into arguments with your clothes, for heaven's sake.

I had a similar problem with tulip-shaped skirts, and you know, whenever I see a woman in a tulip skirt, it always brings to mind images of a snake that has just swallowed a golf ball. Now, who would want that on their fashion mood board?

Rah-rah skirts aren't exactly challenging, and they're not really a trend as they've been around for years, but wearing layers of frills at the top of your thighs will rarely do you any favours. An A-line skirt will give the effect you're probably trying for with the rah-rah – i.e. making your legs look proportionally slimmer – and won't make you look like you're en route to a 'Back to the 80s' party.

Long skirts can look elegant but wear them with a structured or even quite sexy top to balance out the proportions … Of course, you can reverse the proportions and wear a plain short skirt and then a really ruffly top

THE PENCIL SKIRT IS A SHAPE THAT IS GOING TO FLATTER A WOMAN. IT HOLDS EVERYTHING IN, DOESN'T ADD VOLUME AND GIVES A GORGEOUS HOURGLASS SHAPE

The pencil skirt is a shape that is going to flatter a woman. It holds everything in, doesn't add volume and gives a gorgeous hourglass shape I love that 50s silhouette because it's seductive but ladylike, no G-strings falling out of jeans or whatever. And it really is a timeless shape – after all, it's flattered women for the past fifty years! My favourite way to wear it is to make a whole look out of it, kind of sexy secretary, with a fitted masculine shirt, a good bra and some beloved high heels or boots. It's a look that really suits my shape as it gives me some curves, but it also really works on curvier women. Roland Mouret, who probably made the best pencil skirts, once told me that he designs all of his clothes with a size 14 figure in mind and I've seen his clothes work on size 16s as well as size 8 models, proving that it's not just a style for skinny minnies. The fact that he has got to be one of the best-looking designers, I promise, in no way compromised my incorruptible fashion judgement! Alexander McQueen is the other designer who designs amazing pencil skirts – all Hitchcock heroine, very feminine and beautifully made. In his new diffusion line, McQ, McQueen has made some great, affordable ones in denim, giving them a bit more of a youthful kick but still using that classic, slender yet curvy McQueen cut. Otherwise,

Sandals by Jimmy Choo

I sometimes make my own skirts out of long, tassled vintage shawls . . . perfect with flip-flops on the beach during the day or with a vest and pretty sandals for cocktails in the evening

go to high-street stores that aim at the older end of the market as opposed to the more youthful ones, as it is a more mature style.

There are plenty of other skirt styles out there. Paul & Joe and Whistles are good for simple, knee-length, bias-cut skirts. One of my favourite styles is the bell cut, which is basically quite a short skirt cut slightly rounded out, so it falls like a bell around your thighs. Burberry Prorsum, Chloe and Azzedine Alaïa have all done this, and labels like Nanette Lepore have picked up on it as well. Diane von Furstenburg makes pretty, simple skirts that don't wrinkle and last for years; Marc by Marc Jacobs, Eley Kishimoto and Miu Miu are good for sweet little summer skirts with kitsch patterns as well as the occasional long skirt. Zara and Principles have pretty knee-length versions that are good for the office and lunch with your boyfriend's parents.

I sometimes make my own skirts out of long, tasselled vintage shawls, which are brilliant for when you're on holiday as they can double up as evening cover-ups, meaning you get two uses out of one garment. As a skirt, I just pin it up on my hip with a big vintage brooch and it makes a really lovely individualized outfit, perfect with flip-flops on the beach during the day or with a vest and pretty sandals for cocktails in the evening. This kind of shawl is also great as a dress for when you're pregnant as you just wrap it around under your arms and pin it with a brooch. Shawls also really dress up a little black dress, giving a classic more of an original kick.

Speaking of the little black dress, that is obviously an essential every woman should have in her wardrobe. A simple black pencil dress is probably one of the most useful things you can own because you can dress it up in so many different ways and no one will realize you're wearing the same thing over and over – you can wear it with flats for coffee with your girlfriends, you can wear it with heels and pearls. I've had a Dolce & Gabbana one for twelve years that I still wear loads. This brand has always made them brilliantly, particularly their structured, narrow-fitting ones going for that Sicilian widow look they've specialized in since they started out. It is worth considering spending a little more if you can afford to for your classic dress – your LBD and your tweed shift – as these are the dresses that should last you for years and they'll always be in style. Dresses on the high street are great but they are often more trendy than classic, perfect for just one season but not really long-term prospects. Having said that, as previously mentioned, my little one from Miss Selfridge served me pretty well all those years back in the Spice Girls, so occasionally you can get lucky; but you have to set aside the time to hunt one down properly as opposed to doing the usual supermarket sweep on a crowded Saturday afternoon.

The high street is just fantastic for day dresses. In the past ten years the stores have

I always think Kate Moss does date outfits very well: a simple vintage

become so much better at doing prints and colours, both of which really liven up a summer dress. In the 80s and early 90s, their attempts at patterns often looked tacky and heavy-handed. Now, they are much more appealing, probably, I think, because designers on the high street are looking more and more to vintage clothes for inspiration. H&M in particular has started doing really fantastic dresses in delicate, unusual prints that look almost vintage and New Look made one of the most popular dresses of summer 2006 – a gorgeous silken, floral one that flattered everyone. Monsoon has long ones that are great to take on holiday. Primark and, more recently, Peacocks have improved lately to an almost unrecognizable extent compared to their former selves, and both are good at making nice summer dresses at unbelievably good prices.

As well as the high street improving, supermarkets have wisely stepped up their game with fashion and you can pick up some nice day dresses here. Tu at Sainsbury's and George at Asda are both good but the best is probably Florence + Fred at Tesco, which takes very clever tips from the shows each season. About a year ago, they made a long green chiffon dress that was the spitting image of one Chloe had just done and it became one of the most sought-after pieces of the season on the high street! I heard about people driving all around town trying to find it, running into every Tesco they passed and rifling through the rails. On eBay it was being sold for two and even three times its normal price. Now, who'd have ever thought that a supermarket dress would cause such hysteria?

If you're able and willing to spend a little more, Marc by Marc Jacobs does great ones that last for years, as do Sara Berman, Vanessa Bruno, Whistles, Issa or Paul & Joe. Diffusion

dress and scruffy hair, and it looks easy and fabulous . . .

lines by designers for department stores or high-street stores are good hunting grounds for nice day dresses. Many good designers, such as Lulu Guinness, Matthew Williamson, Julien Macdonald and Jasper Conran, have now made diffusion lines for mainstream stores so everybody can get a little piece of a top designer in their closet. When Karl Lagerfeld designed his range for H&M, a friend who bought his black slip dress for less than £20 claims to have worn it to 'every other party I've been to'. Stella McCartney's, also for H&M, was great too.

Little Black

It's worth spending a little more on your <u>Little Black Dress</u> as this is a dress that should last you for years and it'll always be in style

House of Fraser

Belle & Bunty

The high street is just fantastic for day dresses. In the past ten years the stores have become so much better at doing <u>prints and colours</u>, both of which really liven up a summer dress

Print

Sara Berman

Prom dresses have become popular in the past few years and they can look adorable. The best kind to get are ones with 50s prints . . . great for special occasions

Wrap dresses are the ultimate proof of how the best fashion usually comes from the simplest formula. Because the cut is so clean, you can have more fun with patterns and colours

Diane Von Furstenberg

One of the strongest ranges recently was Celia Birtwell's for Topshop, which had some really cute little wafty 70s dresses that just made me want to part my hair down the middle and pose on a Marrakech rooftop.

Some designers have also started making really good-value lines for catalogues, which is obviously extremely convenient if you just don't have the time to trawl the shops. La Redoute, a French mail-order catalogue, is both the best known and the best in that respect. Designers like Karl Lagerfeld, Jean Paul Gaultier and Emanuel Ungaro have made clothes for the company as well as perhaps lesser-known names like Vanessa Bruno and Tomas Maier, who now designs for Bottega Veneta, one of my real favourites when it comes to luxury brands. It is just a fantastic catalogue and with very good service.

Prom dresses have become popular in the past few years and they can look adorable. The best kind to get are ones with 50s prints – mini poodles, for instance – taking the look to the tongue-in-cheek extreme. Great for special occasions. But I will always keep a large space in my wardrobe for simpler shapes: slip dresses and pencil dresses. A simple day dress that skims the legs and hips, has a defined waist and good support for your boobs, is the perfect thing for a weekend lunch out with your husband.

You'll be surprised at how versatile some dresses are: wrap dresses, of course, are the obvious example and I am so pleased they've come back into fashion again. They are the ultimate proof of how the best fashion usually comes from the simplest formula. Because the cut is so clean, you can have a lot more fun with the patterns and colours. This rule, by the way, applies to all clothes: the fussier the garment, the simpler the colour or pattern should be.

Another benefit to the simplicity of wrap dresses is that the high street has been

Wrap dresses . . . the ultimate proof of how the best fashion usually comes from the simplest formula

Flip-flops by
Jimmy Choo

Little cotton dresses with simple flats are perfect for weekend lunches with friends, and are the easiest thing in the world to find on the high street

able to do its own really good versions of this Diane von Furstenburg classic, with special mention to Oasis and Topshop. The West Village in London has also done some great ones. The young and increasingly popular label Issa has also picked up on the style, making them in cute, youthful prints.

Honestly, once you have a wrap dress you really will, as they say, wonder how you managed without. They are the perfect thing for work with a pair of boots, for summer holidays with some flip-flops, and for dates with a fabulous pair of heels. When von Furstenburg first created the wrap dress back in the 70s, it was seen as almost a feminist garment because it gave women such freedom and, thirty years on, I can't think of a more stylish or practical fashion nod to feminism.

Shirt dresses are also very simple. Personally, though, they're not something I wear very often but, if I do, I like to sex them up a little, giving them a bit of a shape, for example with a belt and a fabulous pair of heels. A flirtier variation you can try is an extra-long thin knit (but not too thin!) jumper belted around your hips, but just make sure it really is long enough to be decent. I often do this with David's jumpers for summer evenings.

Vest tops that have been lengthened into little summer cotton dresses are also great, and can be worn on the beach (they are the perfect thing to slip on when you come out of the sea as they dry so quickly) or back at home. C&C California do lovely super-soft ones, and I love Petit Bateau too. And the high street, of course, does them every summer in bright pops of colour.

Dresses in general are amazingly useful, mainly because you can wear the same one in so many different ways by just changing your shoes. Little cotton dresses are one example: with high-heeled sandals they're great for a dinner date, with simple flats they're perfect for weekend lunches with friends, and these really are the easiest thing in the world to find on the high street. Similarly, a jumper dress works in so many situations as it looks smart enough for going out for a nice meal, but not too formal that you couldn't wear it to go shopping with your girlfriends. Wear it with boots and you've got an outfit that is cool without looking like you're trying too hard. They keep you warm – a rare quality in a dress! – and are the perfect thing if you're having a bit of a bloated day before your time of the month. Get one that slips

Flip-flops by Giuseppe Zanotti Design

A JUMPER DRESS WORKS IN SO MANY SITUATIONS ... WEAR IT WITH BOOTS AND YOU'VE GOT AN OUTFIT THAT IS COOL WITHOUT LOOKING LIKE YOU'RE TRYING TOO HARD

off one of your shoulders as that always looks sexy, and one that doesn't have sleeves and is maybe even belted, as jumper dresses can add bulk so it's good to give a sense of your real shape beneath. Stella McCartney – who always does that slouchy but sexy, elegant but effortless style so well – kicked off the trend for jumper dresses and the high street has picked up on it brilliantly. You can even make your own by just taking a long chunky cardigan and belting it up tightly, but do be careful as it's all too easy to then go out and inadvertently show onlookers a bit more than you intended . . .

Empire line dresses are also good for those bloated days, but that's not to say it is a fail-safe style. For a start, a badly cut one – when it doesn't really follow the shape of your body – can easily make you look pregnant, and while there's certainly nothing wrong with this if you actually are pregnant (as a mother of three, I should hope not!) it might not be a look you are going for otherwise. It's also incredibly difficult to pull off if you have any kind of bust whatsoever: the fabric juts out over your boobs and then falls straight down, giving you a really weird cliff-like appearance. Empire-line dresses can look really sweet on women who are relatively flat-chested. There's been a real trend for them recently, and for the similar baby-doll dresses for everyday wear, but as I said, just make sure you get a well-cut one otherwise you'll spend all day having people ask you when it's due!

The perfect date dress is one that gives a hint of sexiness – but just a hint – and shows off the best of your body shape, but is also comfortable so you don't spend the whole evening fidgeting with it and you can concentrate on being sparkly, witty and fabulous. On one of my first dates with David I wore a brown suede dress from Oasis with a round neck and a belt at the waist. I picked it because it was flattering and comfortable and fulfilled my dress criteria — covering my top half but getting my legs out. David still talks today about how much he liked that dress. I always think Kate Moss does date outfits very well: a simple vintage dress and scruffy hair, and it looks easy and fabulous.

A pretty lace dress is good for a date, as it's demure but still gives just a peek of skin. I'm very lucky in that Spain is just brilliant for lace, not least because it has been making it since the Middle Ages. It is still a major industry in this country, with women and children wearing lace veils and dresses for traditional holidays and important events like weddings, and to me they always look so beautiful.

I think my favourite date outfit that I've ever worn was a silk full skirt that puffed out a little, a plain V-neck Joseph jumper, pointy court shoes and smooth glossy hair, trying to go for a bit of a ladylike look. Simple, flattering and really pretty without looking like I'd given it too much thought whereas in reality, of course, I'd planned it all well in advance! Looking effortless is actually fashion code for 'this involved lots of thought' and it is a tragic truth that this generally is the best strategy. But it's only through careful planning that you can achieve that look. Ironic, don't you think?

But this does not mean you should spend every waking hour thinking about your clothes because most of us have to be smart about how we use our time. Being a mother has taught me how not to waste so much time faffing about in the closet every morning any more, simply because I don't have a spare minute. Necessity is the mother of invention and all that, and so, as I said earlier, I multitask, planning outfits while I'm doing something else: getting ready for bed or taking a bath. You can get massively stressed as a mum and often feel you never have any time to yourself, but you do learn how to get things done quicker and often you do them just as well as when you used to spend ages thinking about it.

WHERE TO SHOP

1. A-LINE SKIRTS *Prada, Azzedine Alaïa, Cacharel, Day Birger et Mikkelsen, H&M, Urban Outfitters*

2. TULLE SKIRTS *Sara Berman, Rokit, Topshop*

3. MINISKIRTS *Dolce & Gabbana, Versace, Luella, Karen Millen, Topshop*

4. DENIM MINISKIRTS *Earnest Sewn, H&M, Abercrombie & Fitch*

5. LONG SKIRTS *Hobbs, Topshop, Reiss, H&M, Marc by Marc Jacobs*

6. PENCIL SKIRTS *Alexander McQueen, Karen Millen, Zara*

7. BIAS-CUT SKIRTS *Paul & Joe, Ghost, Whistles*

8. BELL-SHAPED SKIRTS *Burberry Prorsum, Azzedine Alaïa, Chloe, Reiss, Nanette Lepore, Topshop*

9. OFFICE SKIRTS

*Reiss, Zara, Diane von Furstenburg,
The West Village*

10. LBD *Dolce & Gabbana, Roberto
Cavalli, Chanel, Miss Selfridge*

11. SUMMER
DRESSES *Chloe, Diane
von Furstenburg, Issa, Cacharel, Marc
by Marc Jacobs, Reiss, Topshop,
Miss Selfridge, Paul & Joe, H&M,
Primark, Peacocks, Florence
+ Fred, Monsoon*

12. WRAP DRESSES

*Diane von Furstenburg,
Issa, Oasis, French
Connection, Topshop,
Zara, The West Village*

13. JUMPER DRESSES

Stella McCartney, Sonia Rykiel, Topshop

Skirts & Day Dresses

89

Accessories

Knee-high boot by JIMMY CHOO; sunglasses by DVB;
faux pearl necklace by CHANEL; white bag by ROBERTO CAVALLI

FIND ME A WOMAN WHO DOESN'T LOVE ACCESSORIES! THEY'RE LIKE TOYS FOR GROWN-UPS, AREN'T THEY?

THEY PERSONALIZE AN OUTFIT, THEY OFTEN LAST A LOT LONGER THAN CLOTHES AND THEY CAN BE A GOOD, QUICK AND NOT TOO EXPENSIVE TREAT ON DAYS WHEN YOU REALLY NEED ONE. Good shoes and bags, for example, should last you decades, if not longer. I always think it's so cool when you see young women carrying around their grandmother's old Hermès bag: not only are those bags obviously beautiful, but it's as if they're carrying around a piece of their family history with them.

It can be worth spending more on your accessories as you'll tend to use them more than most of your clothes: after all, you'll carry your bag every day whereas you probably won't wear the same dress every day – if you do, you might want to see someone about that. You want a bag that you know won't fall apart on the bus on a rainy day, and for that kind of security you might have to pay just a little bit more. That's why it's smart to spend more on things that rely on cut and quality and that you'll use a lot – like jeans, little black dresses, shoes and handbags – and then save on the simpler, more trend-led pieces that won't last as long. Having said all that, since my days as a teenager, all those centuries ago!, things have begun to change in that respect. There are now some great high-street accessories out there. I advise starting at Accessorize on the high street or, for something a little more expensive but not ridiculously so, Butler & Wilson.

I've always been an accessories junkie. When I was a kid, a friend of my mum's

gave me a Gucci carrier bag after she bought some shoes there. I loved that bag and carried all my school books round in it for ages until the bottom of the bloody thing fell out completely. But it just goes to show how you can personalize your look with some of the most unexpected of accessories and I can't think of anything that says more about me when I was that age than a Gucci carrier bag instead of a school satchel. It also reflects how accessories can be a cheaper and more sensible way of giving you that designer-name fix, and in those days I certainly didn't have much spare cash.

Anyway, I guess it isn't all that surprising that the first designer handbag I ever bought was from, yes, Gucci.

I remember that when I got my first pay cheque from appearing in the musical show *Bertie*, my sister, Louise, and I rushed down to Patrick Cox first thing on a Saturday morning and queued up to buy a pair of Wannabes, which were very much the thing to have then. I didn't have enough to buy two pairs so we bought one, some white slingbacks, to share. I was so proud of those shoes I just wanted to wear them every single day. I probably did, actually, whenever Louise wasn't wearing them herself, of course! And funnily enough, just to show that you can never guess what life's going to bring you, Patrick is now one of my

When I was a kid, a friend of my mum's gave me a Gucci carrier bag after she bought some shoes there. I loved that bag and carried all my school books round in it for ages

friends. When I met him a few years after the Wannabe triumph, that story was one of the first things I told him and he just loved it, proving that designers get as excited about you loving something they've made as you do about buying it.

That, I have to say, has been one of the nicest discoveries I've made since I've started meeting more designers. At a big fashion party recently, I wore a beautiful Roland Mouret dress that just worked so well with my body shape, with a tight top half and then a ballerina-style skirt. Then who do I bump into there but Roland himself! I loved that dress and felt fantastic to be wearing it – it's a real fairytale dress.

Shoes are probably every woman's number one accessory. Maybe it's a Cinderella complex, but there is just such a pleasure to be had in looking down at your feet and seeing something fabulous. Even if you have to wear a sensible suit to the office, you can slip on a pair of really cool or pretty shoes and, during a particularly dull meeting, just tug up your trouser legs, look at them and reassure yourself that you're not turning into some office clone. Do you remember when Theresa May, chairperson of the Tory party, wore those leopard-print shoes to the Tory party conference a few years back? Well, I never thought I'd see something of the kindred spirit in a Tory party chairperson.

The most useful kind you can possibly own is a pair of tan high-heeled shoes, with either pointed toe or open toe. You can buy those from Manolo Blahnik, Christian Louboutin or a store on the high street like Russell & Bromley or Pied A Terre. Not only do they elongate your leg, because it looks as if you're not wearing shoes at all, but they will go with pretty much any outfit and dress it up. So if you're wearing jeans and trainers, you can just kick off your trainers, put on your shoes and your look will totally change and be smartened up for the evening. Just check out how elegant ice skaters are, spinning about in their tan-coloured boots, making their legs look endless.

Bear in mind also that open-toed shoes can elongate your legs as they can give the illusion that the line of your leg goes on forever . . . Of course, you have to be practical sometimes: a woman wearing open shoes in the rain in winter can look ridiculous, especially with muddy puddles gathering between her cold little toes. Fortunately, I don't have to worry about that too much out here in Spain, but it's definitely something to remember in Britain as you're getting dressed in the morning. I wonder if the weather presenters appreciate how much their early-morning words of wisdom affect British women's footwear decisions every day.

At a big fashion party recently, I wore a beautiful Roland Mouret dress. . . Then who do I bump into there but Roland himself! I loved that dress and felt fantastic to be wearing it – it's a real fairytale dress

There are some lovely round-toed shoes about nowadays – Chloe and Marc Jacobs make pretty ones and they've been copied on the high street, with Kurt Geiger in particular doing really fabulous ones.

Round-toed shoes do look good with full knee-length skirts, but I find I just get more wear out of pointy-toed shoes. I also know that pointed shoes give me more of an illusion of height so I instinctively reach for them in my closet.

So, as is often the case, there is no real right or wrong decision – it just comes down to what pair makes you feel better and more confident when you wear them.

Never, ever, buy a pair of shoes that are too small, no matter how much you love them. Remember: if they pinch just a little when you try them on in the shop, imagine what they'll feel like at the end of a working day. You'll just end up never wearing them and feeling very cross with yourself when you see them in the closet every morning. If you have fallen in love with a pair of shoes but the shop doesn't have your size, and if the shoes are closed-toe, go up a size: you can then take them to a cobbler, like Timpsons, and have a pad put in. This won't work, however, if the shoes have ankle straps, as these will just bag around your leg, or, of course, if the shoes are open. In those cases, you're just going to have to live without them.

I've spoken a bit already about ankle straps and how they can truncate the line of your leg. But if you're self-conscious about your ankles, particularly if they tend to swell up during that time of the month, then ankle straps are definitely best avoided because they do draw attention to water retention. T-strap shoes are similarly tricky as they also shorten your legs and can make your feet look wider by splitting them down the middle. Basically, as you now know, I tend to go for the

TO VICTORIA
YOU LOOK AMAZING
IN MY DRESS XXXX?!'E
ROLAND

Love
Richard

simpler, cleaner option and a basic court or sandal is, in my opinion, just the most flattering style. Less fuss is always the best way, in all areas of life, really.

Good boots with a thick wooden heel are another smart buy as you can wear them with jeans, shorts or summer dresses and skirts, giving them a bit of a tougher edge. I really like them with bare legs as they then look very cool but also quite sexy. Now that they are becoming so popular they have become a bit of a high-street staple too. Just look carefully when you buy them because they can look cheap if made badly. To be practical, make sure you get them in leather not suede, as that just turns to mulch in the rain and it's ridiculous to buy a pair of boots that pucker and wilt whenever they get near water. And, unlike suede, leather boots look better as they get older because they take on a worn-in, vintage look.

Boots with too many buckles flying about everywhere look pretty gimmicky now, and I'd recommend giving those pirate-style boots a little rest now because they really have been copied to death. Frankly, they are a little too reminiscent of Michael Jackson, circa *Bad* era, so I'd take a tip from Michael and just keep them in the closet . . .

Speaking of boots, I personally struggle with flat boots. I know, I know, people seem to love them these days, and I've seen a lot of girls wearing them over jeans, but I have yet to be convinced. Karl Lagerfeld makes some fantastically cool ones for Chanel, but they just don't work on me. And is it just me or do all these women wearing narrow flat boots over trousers look like they're off to war?

If you want boots but can't do high heels, why not get a pair with a low, chunky (not kitten, though – we'll discuss this in a minute) heel: they are just as comfortable, and just that bit of a heel really does make enough of a difference.

As for Ugg boots, I wouldn't wear them outside – and I can say that because, as I write this, I am wearing a pair myself! But, well, I am indoors!

Definitely not a good idea to wear flat boots with a tracksuit. If you're to wear a tracksuit, pair it with some clean white trainers for a kinda hip-hop look.

I do like wedges, but it can be hard to make them look sexy as they are so clunky, so you need to get them super-high. And speaking of clunky, there has been a real trend recently for platform wedges after Chloe did some whopping great enormous ones which looked fantastic with shorts and long, wafting dresses for, respectively, pin-up and 70s chick looks. Now, I'm definitely not a platforms girl as I think they can make you look like you've got cement blocks around your ankles and have been captured by the Mafia and are being sent to sleep with the fishes. When I was in the Spice Girls, all the rest of the girls wore those Buffalo boots but I just completely refused. One day, though, I tried on a pair out of curiosity, and to this day I'm amazed the girls were able to dance in them.

So I was a little wary about this wedge-platform thing but I've discovered that if you wear a good pair underneath a super-long pair of jeans or trousers, you won't believe how long your legs look: the wedge platforms basically work like a pair of stilts, just a little more sturdy. Recently, I was persuaded to wear a pair of really beautiful ones and I was completely converted. My legs looked about 10 foot long,

I DO LIKE WEDGES, BUT YOU NEED TO GET THEM SUPER-HIGH OTHERWISE YOUR FEET CAN LOOK CHUNKY, LIKE YOU'VE GOT CEMENT BLOCKS AROUND YOUR ANKLES

which doesn't happen every day. I don't think I took them off the whole weekend. Word of warning: even though wedges are in some ways easier to wear than heels because they cover more surface area and are more supported, wedge platforms are a whole different game. So don't, for example, try to navigate cobblestones or run for a bus in them as you will end up with a scraped knee or a twisted ankle for your pains. Remember that even Naomi Campbell struggled with them, though she managed to carry it off with a supermodel's aplomb. Fabulous!

Platform wedges can be very heavy, so watch that you don't end up dragging your feet and doing that hunched-over walk that just never looks nice.

Canvas wedges by Miu Miu at www.net-a-porter.com
Metallic wedges by Kurt Geiger Fashionistas

One shoe style I have little love for is the kitten heel. I think a lot of women see them as the wearable compromise to high heels, but in fact they have none of the benefits of high heels yet also none of the casual ease of flats. High heels elongate your leg because they pull up your calf muscles; kitten heels make your muscles tense and swell up; high heels hoist you up; kitten heels make you slump. But most of all, they make your feet look bigger: they emphasize the feet by having them point downwards. There is nothing wrong with big feet but in this case they will look out of proportion to the rest of your body. I also always think women wearing kitten heels look as if they're about to go up a stair, which is, I have to say, a rather odd look if you're nowhere near a staircase.

But then, I am a real high-heels girl. Some people can do the whole dressed-up flats look really well – Elle Macpherson, for instance, always looks amazing in flats. The fact that she's a 6-foot goddess may have something to do with it. But if you do love pretty flats, Zara and Topshop do them well, or check out the website www.prettyballerinas.com.

But there is no doubt that the price of wearing high heels is a painful one. In the seventeenth and eighteenth centuries, men used to wear high heels and a part of me wishes they still did because then maybe we girls would get a little more sympathy when we complain about our aching feet. But you can now buy Party Feet by Scholl's, which act like invisible pillows beneath the balls of your feet. They won't make heels completely pain-free but they are a definite improvement and will give

I am a real high-heels girl . . . I like to wear heels up to 11 cms high

you at least an extra hour or so on the dance floor.

I've never really got the whole ballet-pump thing, either. Granted, many people look fantastic in them, but I would just feel like a duck paddling about on the river bank.

If I do wear flats, they tend to be trainers, sandals or flip-flops, and I am quite picky about all of them. Trainers have to be crisp and white Adidas Y3, white Nike Airmax or Bathing Ape, but never dirty ones of any variety. You can also find some really good collectible trainers from Japan. But whatever trainers you have, be careful about wearing them with miniskirts. That whole fly girl look very rarely does anyone any favours.

With sandals, just a pretty, thin-soled pair is perfect for nice summer evenings.

but that's a bit tricky for every day if I'm running around, even I admit

You could go for ones with perhaps one or two aquamarine stones or some gold detailing on the strap over your foot, but don't get too carried away with it. Also, remember that thin soles are always more elegant-looking than heavy, thick ones, though they are more delicate. Happily, however, the shoe-repairing industry has picked up on this problem and places like Timpson can now waterproof the soles but still keep them thin.

Keep the sandals a neutral colour – black, white or, best of all, sand. Summer clothes tend to be more brightly coloured than winter ones so it's just smart to keep your summer shoes subtle. Plus you can then have a little more fun (and I stress, LITTLE) with the decoration on the shoes themselves. Plain ones, though, can look very classy: Peacocks made some fantastic ones last season that were simple, thin-soled and very pretty on the foot, so always keep an eye out for fashion everywhere you shop. Look out for them in Zara too.

As for flip-flops, I know everyone's obsessed with Havaianas and, yes, they do come in good colours and were probably the first flip-flops ever not to rub so painfully between your toes, thanks to their satin-soft rubber. Since the company started forty years ago, 2.2 billion pairs have been sold, meaning they have to be up there with Gisele as one of Brazil's biggest exports.

Flip-flops, by the way, are one summer shoe that you can splash about with bright colours all you like because they're such an easy basic. I will say one thing, though: your feet are often the part of your body that gets the most tan as they're almost always

Flip-flops by Havaianas

BRA 45/46
avaianas
USA 12 EUR 47/48

Flip-flops...one summer shoe that you can splash about with bright colours all you like because they're such an easy basic

out in the sun, and white flip-flops will emphasize your lovely burnished glow.

But, as I keep saying, it's really all about high heels for me. I like to wear heels up to 11 centimetres high but that's a bit tricky for every day if I'm running around, even I must admit.

As for chunky or thin heels, I tend to go for the latter, just because I think they look daintier and more feminine. But there has been quite a trend for chunkiness recently and, yes, they do look pretty cool and can be flattering on your leg, so I have branched out a bit.

The ultimate shoes, as every stylish woman knows, are a pair of high-heeled Manolo Blahniks. I actually happened to meet Mr Blahnik earlier this year at a big fashion event in New York and I was completely star-struck.

On the high street, Topshop really stands out. It has high heels that look very much like designer and vintage versions with interesting detailing, such as satin bows and delicate buckles. Their boots, too, are usually brilliant, sometimes made with almost vintage-looking leather so it looks like you got them from the coolest vintage shop around, but make sure you waterproof them as soon as you buy them. They have also started doing pretty, thin-soled flats with piping and other details, which are very cheap and so great with miniskirts or under jeans.

You'll find a great variety of Topshop shoes and boots in its Oxford Circus branch and its shoe outlet in Manchester. However, with most high-street shops, you often have to go to the flagship stores, which are generally in central London, to get the best stuff, and it just seems a shame for anyone who doesn't live in London.

Shelly's is another high-street shoe store that has come on in leaps and bounds, making some very beautiful two-tone party shoes in jewel-coloured velvet, and adorable little flats. Very Bottega Veneta, one of my favourite labels for accessories, but sadly costing an arm, a leg and all the rest of your body too – unlike Shelly's, thankfully. Kurt Geiger is another really, really good store, especially their new Fashionistas range, which is a little pricier than their usual selection but does look so much like some of the best stuff you can get from designers. Their boots and heels really last for years, and the assistants who work in their shops are always, I've found, very knowledgeable and helpful. New Look and Bertie do some fun and quirky party shoes, and Zara does great high-heel basics.

Karen Millen can make some great high-heeled party shoes that are strikingly similar to the ones on the catwalks. They do occasionally go over the top with dangly bits and enormous ankle ties, but sometimes they are genuinely very pretty and look like they ought to cost five times more. Best of all, they last for ever. Faith, too, is a good hunting ground for party shoes. Marks & Spencer can also do some extremely good shoes, which some people might not expect, but they are a real fashion editor's secret. You have to look past the clunky little orthopaedic-looking shoes that for some reason always seem to be at the front of their display, but you'll find really pretty little heels that are perfect for work or nights out. Their wedges last summer were excellent and very fun in a 50s sort of way. Finally, Pied A Terre really picked up on the chunky-heel trend recently and have been making very Chloe-esque sandals and heels for, obviously, about a fifth of the price.

If you're willing and able to spend more for special-occasion shoes, aside from Manolo, I really recommend Christian Louboutin, who makes probably the sexiest heels you can find, and I love the way the soles of the shoes are always red, giving a little flash of scarlet as you walk. Roberto Cavalli, Jimmy Choo and Dolce & Gabbana shoes are always pretty and feminine, and Prada ones last for years. Lulu Guinness has started making really cute ones that are as pretty and detailed as her bags. I particularly like how inside some of them she has written 'You have to suffer to be beautiful', which gives them a touch of the Ronseal advert, doing exactly what they say on their tins.

I really recommend
Christian Louboutin
. . . I love the way
the soles of the shoes
are always red,
giving a little flash of
scarlet as you walk

Heels by Christian Louboutin

I DON'T KNOW ANY WOMAN WHO ISN'T A BIT OF A BAG LADY, IN THE FASHION SENSE, OF COURSE. . .

BUT WOMEN STARTED USING BAGS ONLY IN THE NINETEENTH CENTURY; BEFORE THAT THEY JUST KEPT ALL THEIR BITS AND BOBS DANGLING FROM THEIR WAIST OR TUCKED IN POCKETS, AN IDEA THAT WOULD SEEM PRETTY IMPOSSIBLE TO MOST OF US GIRLS NOW, CONSIDERING THE AMOUNT WE CART ABOUT THESE DAYS. After many hours of practice, I've mastered the art of fitting baby wipes, a nappy and a credit card into a little Fendi bag (it's all about careful rolling techniques, you see, just tucking things inside each other and then rolling it all up in the nappy) and maybe a lipstick if I'm being particularly clever. I then pack David out with all of my make-up and extra bits, as if he's some undercover spy, and I'm good to go. I may be a mummy but I still want to look nice! After all, just because you have kids doesn't mean that you have to go all mumsy and frumpy and carry big plastic-coated bags covered with little bunnies everywhere you go. You don't suddenly lose your personality and all taste as soon as you leave the hospital delivery room, you know! I mean, keeping your sense of style does not negate your abilities as a mother. If anything, it can actually be a help because feeling good about how you look will make you a happier, more confident person, two very important qualities for a mother to pass on to her children.

For an everyday bag, I admit, I tend to use quite a big bag, mainly because I have all the kids' stuff to cart about so if I just have some tiny, dinky little thing I inevitably end up just carrying multiple bags to cope with the overspill. A good

Bag by Topshop Vintage

everyday bag should have a separate pocket inside in which you can keep your keys, phone, ipod and a little mirror for emergency make-up and post-lunch, spinach-in-the-teeth moments. In fact, I got so fed up with not being able to find a decent bag in which I could carry all the kids' stuff and still look good that I designed one myself for a Japanese company – Samantha Thavasa. This has been a huge success because not only is it practical, it looks cool. I kept it in very simple plain colours, with plenty of small pockets to separate out bottles and other baby essentials and a special changing mat attached to the outside. There's been a real trend recently for having the pockets sit on the outside of the bag, thanks to Mulberry's amazingly popular Roxy bag, which has its chunky pockets on the bag's exterior. Alternatively, there are some very suave-looking bags around that have subtle pockets on the outside but instead of looking chunky and sitting on top of the bag the pockets are hidden on the inside, with only their zipper on the bag's front, if you see what I mean, so it's still easy to find your essentials, but the bag's shape is kept simple and sleek.

Another thing you must look for in a bag is that it closes properly. So many bags just flap open, making it far too easy for pickpockets. One that zips properly or has various buckles criss-crossing the top will work. Just don't get one of those sloppy shopper bags as they are the thief's best friend. Good places for proper big day bags include Burberry, Prada, Marc Jacobs, Mulberry, Jimmy Choo, Chloe, Hermès, Anya Hindmarch, Fendi, Balenciaga and, on the high street, Gap, Urban Outfitters and Orla Kiely.

Topshop's Vintage range is particularly brilliant for bags. A friend of mine once found a really gorgeous Dior satchel bag there for only £50 and it has lasted for years.

But satchel bags can be a little tricky. On the plus side, satchels can give certain people a real cool, urban or boho kind of look, and they do leave your arms free, which is always a relief. Designers like Roberto Cavalli make beautiful ones and you can get cute ones on the high street that look almost vintage. Mulberry do good ones too.

The Elgin bag
by Mulberry

Satchels can give certain people a real cool, urban or boho kind of look

However, they can also look a little too casual, so you really have to look at what you're wearing to see if it goes. If you're going to a formal event, or are wearing anything A-line, the satchel really won't work because, in the case of the A-line, it will totally crush down the line of your skirt or dress. Also, if you overload your bag it will drag down on your shoulder and that does no one's posture any favours. But, most of all, you have to be reasonably small-busted to carry off the satchel as the strap cuts right across your front, squashing you down and giving you three boobs. This is why I actually think they best suit men (the ones without boobs, that is): David, for example, looks great with a satchel bag, better than most of us women, really.

If you truly love your shoulder bags, and they're just more practical for your everyday life, the best sort to get are the big ones with short straps that hang right under your armpit. They give a cool 70s, almost *Avengers* kind of look to your outfit, and they work with jeans and skirts, plus they are better in terms of keeping your belongings safe. But the problem with these, like most shoulder bags, is that they can be difficult to wear with a winter coat, which is just too bulky for the strap. They also aren't totally secure as people often tuck them behind their back to keep them out of the way. Instead, I almost always opt for handbags which, like a lot of women, I just jam up to my elbow to free up my hands, like the Queen. You can find these at Luella and, on the high street, Oasis.

Structured handbags look more formal and proper and are generally more timeless, whereas soft ones – the famous 'Paddington' by Chloe, for example – tend to be a bit cooler, younger and fashion-y. So it just depends on the look you're going for as both have their advantages. Structured handbags really came into fashion in the 50s when Grace Kelly was photographed for the cover of *Life* magazine with a Hermès bag, which was quickly named the Kelly bag (and are now really sought-after and collectible). Kelly was also a fan of Valextra bags and if you can't trust Grace Kelly for bag inspiration, who can you trust? Hermès still makes some of the best structured bags, and Asprey and Luella do gorgeous ones too. Burberry's day bags are really roomy and fabulous. At a less high price, there's Russell & Bromley, and Marks & Spencer can do some good ones. One of the first presents David ever bought me was a gorgeous black Prada handbag, delivered to my parents' home with a massive bouquet of roses. A fabulous bag, of course, but there are other reasons why that one will always be one of my favourites.

When buying satchels, structured bags and softer ones, particularly ones in beautiful leather, you can find a fantastic selection in vintage markets, especially Portobello, Spitalfields and Brighton, and often they are much cheaper than you get on the high street.

For dressier events, I'll always go for a clutch bag; they aren't practical at all but are just so beautiful, and at parties I do let myself choose beauty over practicality. They were particularly popular in the 30s and 40s and their prettiness has kept them in fashion ever since. You can get some gorgeous, cheaper ones in vintage and second-hand stores, as clutch bags have been very popular for a few years. The high street sometimes has some nice ones, especially at Accessorize, Monsoon, Warehouse and Oasis. If you want to spend more, Lulu Guinness does some of the most beautiful ones ever, notably her famous fan one that really does look like a fan until you see the little zipper at the top. As for designers, Yves Saint Laurent always makes very striking clutches, as does Marni.

Canvas is a good alternative to leather for bags: it's classic but a little bit different. As it is such an American preppy look, it's the preppy American companies, like

Land's End or Kate Spade, that do them particularly well, but, of course, you can find canvas bags pretty much anywhere in the world now; even designers such as Miu Miu and Hermès use canvas, often mixing it with other materials, like wood and leather respectively. The problem is, though, that canvas stains very easily, and if, for example, you have a leaky bottle of baby milk inside your bag, within two seconds your bag will have a bloody great big milk stain sitting on the front, so look out for the potential leakage factor of anything you put in your canvas bag.

I'll often go for leather, ideally brown and a little bit vintage or worn-looking. But as soon as you get your leather bag, make sure you spray it properly with a good, non-staining leather protector, like Collonil's Waterstop, which you can get in any decent leather-goods shop, as otherwise a sudden downpour of rain will ruin your beautiful bag, making it pucker and change colour. Spain, luckily for me, is great for leather goods, particularly its home-grown luxury brands like Loewe as well as the items from the little artisan shops you can find all over the country.

Quilted leather always looks good. The obvious designer reference is Chanel, whose quilted leather handbags have become iconic. Marc Jacobs now quilts some of his bags too, as does Balenciaga, giving this classic look a bit of a younger kick, and high-street stores such as Principles have followed their lead well.

With the exception of Louis Vuitton or Fendi, I can't say I'm really a fan of logoed bags. I have given them a go in my time but they never really work for me, I find. At least Louis Vuitton's monogrammed look is so traditional in the original brown and burnished-orange tones, but most others just seem over the top and get very tired very quickly, and also a bit designer-designer, as I said before. So try not to go for anything too flashy as it becomes too much of a statement. If you really want to put down a lot of money for a bag, go for something more classic and of good quality, that you can use repeatedly and with lots of different outfits. As I've got older I've noticed I've started thinking more and more about what I can wear with what and in a thoroughly good way it has begun to affect the choices I make when I shop, pushing me towards the classic pieces and straight past the kitschy ones.

I just throw on the Chanel sunglasses, which really do, as the fashion magazines say, hide a multitude of sins

As you all know, the crucial accessory for me is a good pair of sunglasses. If you've ever wondered why I'm always wearing them it's very simple: as a mum, I often don't get that much sleep, I don't always have time to put on the Touche Eclat in the mornings, and who can be bothered putting on eyeshadow first thing in the day anyway? So, instead, I just throw on the Chanel sunglasses, which really do, as the fashion magazines say, hide a multitude of sins. There's nothing that ruins the effect of a good outfit faster than puffy, bleary eyes.

This is why I often tend to go for sunglasses with dark or mirrored lenses. Make sure they're a good quality lens with UV to protect your eyes.

You have to try lots of different styles to find one that suits your face. I tend to go with bigger frames as I find smaller ones can give me racoon eyes. Small sunglasses also remind me of Knight Rider and that whole 80s look and, really, there are some styles from the 80s that should just stay in the 80s. Aviators, another throwback, but one which I love, are similarly hit and miss as they can drag down your face if they are too heavy – it all depends on your face shape. If they work on you, go for Raybans, which, of course, is the brand most closely associated with aviators. But the point is, set aside some proper time to try on as many pairs as possible in the shop. Vintage stores and even car-boot sales are great for finding a unique pair of sunglasses in pretty much any size ever imagined and they're often cheaper than anywhere else. Plus, because they're vintage, and therefore by definition at least a few years old, you know they must be of pretty good quality and should last, unlike so many modern sunglasses you find today. Whenever I go to vintage shops with my friends Ben and Maria Louise, we all have such a laugh trying on amazing pairs. Seriously, I have pulled some impressive 70s rock-star looks in my time in some of those shops.

But, as long as you don't let yourself get carried away, you can find some great sunglasses in vintage shops and from vintage makes like Linda Farrow. Linda Farrow first designed glasses back in the 70s and consulted for major brands like Balenciaga and Pucci. The company was only recently relaunched when her son discovered loads of original 70s and 80s sunglasses in the company's warehouse. I've also started designing my own range – well, it makes sense seeing how sunglasses and I have become synonymous! It's been so interesting learning how to design sunglasses properly. For example, frames should be fabulous but also wearable, and you have to get the balance right between oversized and practical. I love my decorated frames but

Sunglasses frames should be fabulous but also wearable, and you

you have to keep the embellishment subtle otherwise you can look a bit clownish instead of classic. It's been so much fun designing my glasses, which are inspired by icons such as Jackie O, Diana Rigg and, of course, Audrey Hepburn.

People sometimes feel timid about experimenting with frames, with images of Timmy Mallett dancing through their heads. But wearing something slightly different from your basic black can actually be really successful. If you're wearing blue or green, lilac ones will work well with your outfit. The sunglasses in Marc Jacobs' new range often come with red and white frames, giving you a fun 70s look, and big white ones are great if you always regretted missing out on the 60s. Spitfire glasses, that you find in Topshop and on Portobello, manage to tread the line between unique and wearable.

Hats are another accessory I often use to hide any less than perfect features on a bad day. Baseball hats, which you can find all over the place in England these days, are a particular favourite of mine as they're so useful if you can't be bothered to do your hair and you just want to bung it up, out of sight. They tend to work best on heart-shaped faces as they can elongate long faces and make them look a little horsey, but, generally, they suit most people. Be careful to get a good shape – not one that looks like it's been run over.

Slogans on caps are OK, and I know I have worn some in my time, but plain ones usually work best as then you can just wear them with anything and not worry about

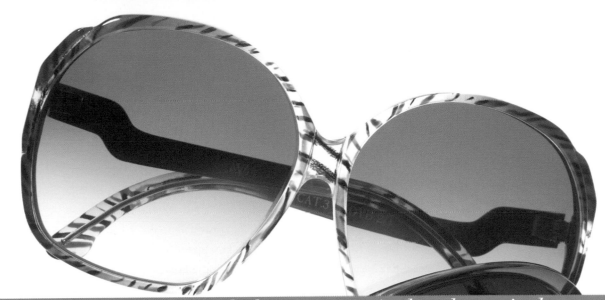

have to get the balance right between oversized and practical

Sunglasses by DVB

it. Also, as with sloganned T-shirts, you tend to be able to wear sloganned caps only a few times before people start to get annoyed with having that same phrase staring back at them every time they look your way. As to whether only people under a certain age should wear baseball caps in general, well, I was talking about this just

I think Philip Treacy does the most innovative and exciting hats. Some of them . . . seem to defy gravity, spiralling up from your scalp

the other day with my mum. 'Oh, definitely,' she said. 'I think past a certain point they just look silly on people.' 'Yeah, you're right,' I said. 'You probably shouldn't wear them once you're over thirty.' She then looked at me, thirty-two and counting, and said, 'What age did you say was the limit?' And I quickly went, 'Um, I meant thirty-five!' So the conclusion is, yes, there probably is a limit but, as is always the case with fashion, rules can be bent.

Cowboy hats are also useful and I have worn them instead of beach hats, which can be pretty naff. If you do prefer a traditional beach hat, go for a plain straw one with an extra-big floppy rim for a dramatic Hollywood diva look. You can find these at Accessorize, Gap or Anya Hindmarch.

Recently, I got some great cowboy hats from a vintage shop but they didn't smell too hot on the inside, I have to say – very eau de sweaty cowboy, which might have worked on Brokeback Mountain, but definitely did not on my head. But, potential odours aside, they are great for covering up sweaty hair, and also protect your hair from getting bleached out by the sun and going all frizzy. They have become much more popular these days and you can now find them all over the high street.

Pretty vintage-style hats can really work, as long as you're willing to pull a bit of a look, i.e. work it with your outfit and have people take a little more notice of you, instead of just slinging on the hat and forgetting about it. For example, you can find really pretty little hats with netting that covers the top half of your face, which look very dramatic. You often find these in vintage shops and even Topshop occasionally does their own versions. But they are, as I said, a bit of a look and really work best for special occasions when you're all done up with an amazing pencil skirt and a monster pair of heels.

For smart occasions, hats can really make an outfit. Just think of all those great photos from the 40s in *Vogue* and *Harper's Bazaar*, with models posing in fabulous full-length gowns and incredible sculptured hats. For inspiration, just look at any shoots in old *Vogue* magazines – particularly those by Norman Parkinson – which you can often find in second-hand bookstores and vintage shops. Today, I think Philip Treacy does the most innovative and exciting hats. Some of them are almost acrobatic in that they seem to defy gravity, spiralling up from your scalp. He made the hat I wore to Buckingham Palace when David received his OBE and although I might not be able to compete with the Queen in terms of regal headware, I did feel I was pulling my weight in that department.

Probably the prettiest way to disguise a bad-hair day is with a headscarf tied over your head and then at the back of your neck. You could go for a vintage Pucci (or Pucci-esque, as the high street has started to do) one. This is one of the few times when I think patterns really work, mainly because it's such a small accessory and therefore the pattern doesn't seem too over-whelming. It makes sense to get your pattern fix just by relegating it to a headscarf. Alternatively, really thick headbands look great, and I always rely on these when I ski to keep my hair from blowing in my eyes and blinding me. You can find them in sportswear shops, like JJB Sports, or else in dance and exercise wear shops, like sweatyBetty or Boots and Claire's Accessories.

You can find really cute hair accessories on the high street now, like feathered combs, hair sticks (those things that look like chopsticks that you stick through a bun) and pretty little hair clips. Things like these not only help to tidy up your hair but distract onlookers from noticing if your hair is looking a bit on the greasy side that day.

EVERYBODY HAS A BAD-HAIR DAY ONCE IN A WHILE AND THAT'S WHY I THINK WEARING YOUR HAIR UP CAN BE THE SAFER OPTION

Designers also do really fun little hair accessories and, although they are undeniably more expensive, they not only look amazing but they really do last for ever. Louis Vuitton makes fun hairbands dangling with chunky gold cubes with LV written on them, and Luella has done some great ones too. Cherry Chau does fabulously over-the-top hair pieces that are great for special occasions. Miu Miu and Prada make some really pretty Alice bands, particularly feathered ones which give a fabulous 20s look to any outfit, however cheap or old the dress. I like Alice bands and it's cool how a glittery and colourful one – which, thanks to inspiration taken from Miu Miu, you can get on the high street – livens up just a jeans-and-vest outfit and does not look out of place. Even a simple plastic one in just a solid bright colour, like red or blue, can really spark up a look.

The truth is, everybody has a bad-hair day once in a while and that's why I think wearing your hair up can be the safer option, particularly in the summer when everyone's hair can look flat and greasy by the end of the day.

Even if you don't live in a country with Spanish-style heat, pulling your hair up into a high, sleek ponytail with a simple black band just looks more pulled together than having it fly about your face.

Small shoulder shawls can be really pretty, particularly embellished ones. It used

A good high-street shop for inexpensive jewellery is Agatha, which has some beautiful vintage-style earrings and pretty little things

Necklace by Agatha

to be that you could only find them in vintage shops but, as with a lot of vintage pieces, the high street has picked up on them and you can find pretty ones all over the place now. Look out for shops that mix vintage pieces with their own collection: Paul & Joe does this well and Coco Ribbon sources very feminine and beautiful vintage pieces alongside more recent bits and bobs. Beaded shawls pinned around your shoulders with a brooch look great over a vest top. I recently went to the stunning vintage shop, Virginia, in west London, run by the equally stunning owner, Virginia. That shop is such a candy store for girls, with original 20s and 30s dresses draped across antique beds. I was supposed to be looking for a full-length dress for an upcoming event but I was completely distracted by one of the most beautiful shawls I've ever seen: black and trimmed with silver beads. I pinned it round the top of a black tulle skirt I also found in the store, giving the look a bit of Spanish flair. That's one of the great joys of accessories: you can really play with them, make looks your own and find new ways of wearing them.

Generally, I'm not really one for wearing lots of jewellery every day – maybe a ring that David gave me. I rarely wear necklaces because I find they can sometimes hang somewhat awkwardly on my bust. If I do, I'll go for a shortish one that stops above my boobs, or a long one that hangs down between my cleavage, which looks sexy.

If you wear jewellery, just watch out that you're not going OTT. It's almost never a good look to pile it on, although pearls are an exception to this rule: just look back to *Breakfast at Tiffany's* to see how beautiful it looks to have multistrands of pearls draped around your wrist and on a choker; Carrie in *Sex and the City* did this really well too. Of course, pearls are expensive, especially if you get the highest-quality ones from places like Asprey. But you can find excellent paste ones on the high street.

You can get some fantastic costume jewellery on the high street now. Marks & Spencer has great rings and earrings, and labels like Freedom and Mikey make fun fashion pieces that last for ages and are really reasonable. New Look always has great, colourful pieces. At Johnny Loves Rosie and Erickson Beamon you will find truly excellent vintage-style brooches and hair pieces, and I've found some great little decorative combs and dramatic earrings and chokers on the high street. Big chunky beads are good for a dramatic look, but wear them sparingly. For really special pieces, I tend to look towards Cavalli, Asprey and Chopard.

Flesh-coloured stockings with fake seams going up the back ...are very alluring

A good high-street shop for inexpensive jewellery is Agatha, which has some beautiful vintage-style earrings and pretty little things. You don't have to spend a fortune to create a fabulous look. My favourite piece of jewellery in the world is a necklace the kids made me as a present out of bits of foam, which I doubt very much I'll ever actually wear but I know I'll always treasure. Similarly, it's the pieces of jewellery from David that will always mean so much more than anything anyone else could ever give me. Jewellery is very pretty, but I find that it's only really exciting if it has a special person or story behind it.

One piece of jewellery I do wear almost every day is a watch. Get either a good man-sized one, or a really pretty delicate one for dressing up. For the former, I really love Jacob & Co, De Grisogono or vintage Rolexes from second-hand stores and, for the latter, Tiffany is the ultimate although the high street has started to make its own beautiful versions. I do think it's best to get one either from the high street or a proper watchmaker.

Moving on to hoisery, a lot of people have got into the whole Prada-esque cashmere ribbed-stockings trend, and they can look good on some people. The best tights labels are Wolford, Falke, Fogal, Jonathan Aston and Jonelle, all of which last for ever; both John Lewis and Selfridges have a really wide selection. But, to be honest, tights in general just make me feel itchy and claustrophobic. Admittedly, I am spoiled, living out here in sunny Spain, but even when I was hanging out in London, I never was one for getting excited over a pair of woolly tights.

I do love fishnet stockings, though, and you can either wear them in a seductive, burlesque way, or give them more of a demure but still sexy look with a pencil skirt. The best are probably from Agent Provocateur. They tend to last that little bit longer

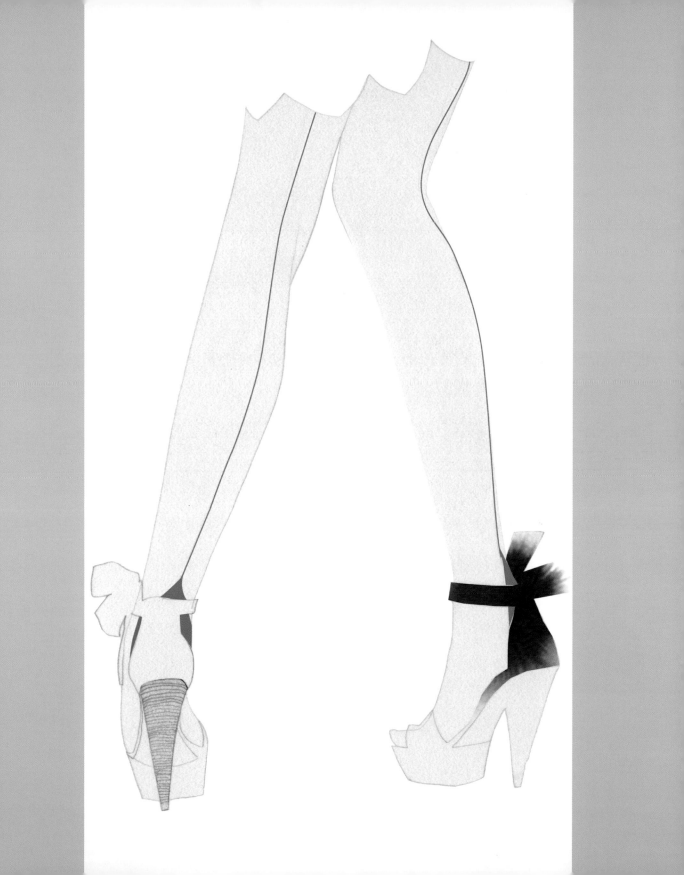

It might seem a bit surprising that I have tattoos — four, to be precise:

and come in great shades. You can also get them from Marks & Spencer or Topshop. I like both big and little fishnet but I recommend sticking with either black or flesh-coloured. Brightly coloured fishnets are a bit too much of a look for my taste. Very Camden Market, and that's often true of brightly coloured tights of any style.

Flesh-coloured stockings with fake seams going up the back, which you can often get from Jonathan Aston, are very alluring. They really are quite fabulous as that seam looks so seductive disappearing up your skirt, and very 30s. At £20 they are pretty expensive but I have to say they do seem to last.

Considering that I tend to advise erring on the minimal side when it comes to accessories and general personal decoration, it might seem a bit surprising that I have tattoos – four, to be precise: on my back, on my neck and on my wrists. I would urge you to really think carefully if you're even considering getting one done. Getting them removed is a painful process and often leaves a scar. But I love all of my tattoos because each of them means something very special to me, and if something has an emotional value then you'll never regret it. For example, for a recent wedding anniversary, David and I got tattooed with the same inscription of love in Hebrew, on my neck and on his arm, which was so romantic, though I have to say it was bloody painful. The five stars on my back represent me and David and each of the kids. They also mean I can survive three months in a freezer, which is handy. And one of the tattoos on my wrist is DB, for David Beckham – or maybe David Blaine, or possibly David Blunkett. I'll leave it up to the tabloids to decide.

on my back, on my neck and on my wrists . . . I love all of my tattoos

WHERE TO SHOP

1. COURT SHOES *Manolo Blahnik, Christian Louboutin, Roberto Cavalli, Pied A Terre, Russell & Bromley*

2. ROUND-TOED SHOES *Chloe, Marc Jacobs, DSquared^2, Topshop, Kurt Geiger, Shelly's, Zara*

3. CHUNKY BOOTS *Dolce & Gabbana, Chloe, Anna Sui, Frye, Shelly's, Office, Topshop*

4. WEDGES & PLATFORMS *Chloe, Marc by Marc Jacobs, Office*

5. TRAINERS *Adidas, Bathing Ape, Nike*

6. SUMMER SANDALS *Manolo Blahnik, Jimmy Choo, Christian Louboutin, Miu Miu at www.net-a-porter.com, L K Bennett, Kurt Geiger, Office, Peacocks, Zara*

7. FLIP-FLOPS *Havaianas available at Office, Gap, Topshop*

8. PARTY SHOES *Manolo Blahnik, Jimmy Choo, Christian Louboutin, Miu Miu at www.net-a-porter.com, Russell & Bromley, Gina, L K Bennett, Kurt Geiger, Office, Shelly's, Kurt Geiger, Karen Millen, Bertie, Faith*

9. DAY BAGS *Burberry, Marc Jacobs, Chloe, Mulberry, Hermès, Balenciaga, Orla Kiely, Anya Hindmarch, Gap, Topshop, vintage markets*

10. SATCHEL BAGS *Roberto Cavalli, Mulberry, Topshop, vintage markets*

11. EVENING BAGS *Roberto Cavalli, Chanel, Lulu Guinness, Anya Hindmarch, Fendi, Accessorize, Topshop, Warehouse*

12. HANDBAGS *Asprey, Hermès, Luella, Chanel, Russell & Bromley, Marks & Spencer, Topshop*

13. CLUTCHES *Lulu Guinness, Fendi, Accessorize, Monsoon, Warehouse, Oasis*

14. SUNGLASSES *Vintage stores, Linda Farrow, Topshop, Gucci, Dolce & Gabbana, Chanel, Topshop*

15. COWBOY HATS *Vintage stores, H&M, Miss Selfridge, Topshop*

16. BEACH HATS *Anya Hindmarch, Accessorize, Gap*

17. HEADBANDS *sweatyBetty, Topshop, Boots, Claire's Accessories*

18. HAIR PIECES *Prada, Miu Miu at www.net-a-porter.com, Louis Vuitton, Cherry Chau, H&M, Oasis, Accessorize, Topshop*

19. MINI SHAWLS *Vintage stores, Paul & Joe, Oasis, Topshop, Coco Ribbon*

20. PARASOLS *Vintage stores, markets, Coco Ribbon, Topshop*

21. JEWELLERY *Asprey, Chopard, De Grisogono, Roberto Cavalli, Agatha, Johnny Loves Rosie, Pebble, Butler & Wilson, Solange Azagury-Partridge, EC One, Fiona Knapp, Accessorize, Freedom, Mikey, Topshop*

18. TIGHTS *Jonathan Aston, Wolford, Falke, Fogal, Jonelle, Marks & Spencer, Agent Provocateur, John Lewis, Selfridges*

Parties

Silver shoes by CHRISTIAN LOUBOUTIN;
Vintage chainmail bag from a selection at BEYOND RETRO

GETTING DRESSED FOR RED-CARPET EVENTS CAN BE A PERILOUS AFFAIR . . .

GENERALLY, I RECOMMEND CHOOSING A CLASSIC DRESS IN A SIMPLE SHAPE, AND THAT'S A GOOD FORMULA TO BEAR IN MIND FOR ANY FORMAL PARTY, PARTICULARLY ONE WHERE YOU KNOW YOU'LL BE PHOTOGRAPHED. If I'm going to a red-carpet event I'll always go direct to the designers to find the dress myself. Also, I am in the incredibly privileged position of being friends with Roberto Cavalli and I'll ring him and explain exactly the sort of dress I want, describing the shape, the colour and the back, as that way it always has my individual stamp on it. For example, Roberto and I worked very closely together on the dress I wore to Elton John's wedding as I wanted something special for that. I loved that dress and still do when I look at the photos.

As I've said before, I don't have a stylist outside of professional fashion shoots because I really enjoy creating the look myself. I remember when I was young I'd go round to a friend's house before a party and we'd be running around, make-up brushes flying about everywhere, and I still try to recreate that today when I can. Before Elton's wedding, for example, two friends came over to help me get ready and just basically have a bit of a laugh all together while swanking it up, and that was really brilliant. But, generally, I don't have the luxury to spend too long getting ready for a party because I like to make the kids' dinner, give them a bath and put them to bed all before I go out, which doesn't leave a lot of time for faffing about with an eyelash comb.

However, if it's a big night out, I'll get my hair properly blow-dried, and that usually takes about forty minutes. Otherwise, I'll just wash my hair myself and then walk around the house in my old-lady curlers, which is what I call those heated

*And Cinderella
did go to the ball.
Dress by Elie Saab*

Having a bit of music on in the background always helps to get you in the

rollers that you just bung in your hair. I don't think I could live without my little old-lady rollers. My sister once bought me a pair of travel hair straighteners, which you can use en route to the party if you're very strapped for time. Be careful as they can really damage your hair, leaving you with charred split ends, which is only a good party look on Halloween.

Then I'll spend about ten minutes on my make-up – by now I have it down to a well-practised art. Having a bit of music on in the background always helps to get you in the mood after a long day and, personally, I tend to go for anything from Frank Sinatra to r 'n' b.

As for the outfit, I always plan it the night before to save more time and also because I hate making rushed decisions as that's when mistakes tend to happen. But I've found that, as you get older, you do know yourself better, and know what really suits you, so you tend not to make silly choices quite so often.

I almost always ask my sister, Louise, and my mum what they think of my outfit. You have to ask the opinion of someone who's close to you, because you can ask loads of people what they think and they'll say, 'Oh, it's wonderful, it's wonderful,' when in actual fact you look rubbish but they either don't want to be rude or just don't know how to tell you. But no one will be more honest with you than your mum or your sister, and they won't let you go out looking ridiculous. Men are pretty good at giving opinions on clothes but I do think it's important to get a woman's point of view too because they're often the ones who will understand what you're trying to do with an outfit and give good, more sympathetic advice, such as: don't show too much skin if you're trying to look sexy. Whereas, although men are useful for not letting you go too far with a look, they will usually tell you that you look fine just to make you hurry up.

My kids are always happy to offer opinions when I get dressed and, as I'm the only woman in the house, they find it really exciting. They're also really good at noticing things, like a new haircut or a new dress, so sometimes you can find advice in the most unexpected of places. But be warned: kids can be brutally honest too, so brace yourself before soliciting their opinions...

mood after a long day . . . I go for anything from Frank Sinatra to r 'n' b

Roberto Cavalli

Roberto Cavalli

With Roberto Cavalli at the Full Length and Fabulous party in 2006

Cruella de Vil!

The 7th Annual White
Tie and Tiara Ball

Roberto Cavalli

I am grateful for the possibility of being close to such a wonderful woman as Victoria for she is not only glamorous and beautiful but a person with a special sensibility, personality and true soul

ROBERTO CAVALLI

I've never been one of those people who tries to make a statement by looking really scruffy and I find it very disappointing if I'm at a big party and some people just look as if they haven't even bothered to make an effort

I do love wearing long dresses. There are so few occasions when you can really dress up, so if one comes along I think it's a wasted opportunity to pass it up. I also think it's more respectful to the person who's throwing the party – I've never been one of those people who tries to make a statement by looking really scruffy and I find it very disappointing if I'm at a big party and some people just look as if they haven't even bothered to make an effort.

Of all the party dresses I've worn so far, my favourite was the Roberto Cavalli Ming Vase print dress that I wore to one of Elton's parties a few years ago. David picked it out and I'd never worn anything like it before. I wanted it to give me a real hourglass shape so when I was getting it fitted I kept asking the seamstresses to pull it tighter, tighter, and they were all saying to me in their Italian accents, 'If we make it any tighter, you won't be able to sit down!' I said, 'I don't care, I'll go in a horsebox standing up if I have to – I want it tighter!' As you can see, party clothes are the one area where my sense of practicality goes out of the window. Anyway, at the party I needed to go to the toilet and I said to David, 'Can you come with me as I won't be able to do up the dress when I come out.' So when I came out, he started to do the dress back up again and the zipper broke! All because I insisted on having it so tight! So there I was, standing with my dress half undone and I just thought, 'Oh, my God! What am I going to do? How embarrassing!' Suddenly, this girl came over with some safety pins and she got right down on her knees and started pinning me in. 'Just a minute, just a minute, almost there!' she was saying, scrambling about on the ground while David held the top of my dress. Well, you'll never believe it, but it wasn't until she stood up and I could see her properly that I realized it was Joss Stone! The moral

*Please don't
fall out!*

141

The most important thing to remember if you're wearing a dress that won't let

of the story is, listen to seamstresses when they tell you that you're making the dress too tight. But if you don't listen . . . never go to a party without safety pins. And I really do always have them on me now.

The most important thing to remember if you're wearing a dress that won't let you wear a bra, such as one with a low back or, in particular, a deep-plunge front, is to make sure you have lots of toupee tape to keep everything in place. There is nothing worse than seeing someone with a boob hanging out or their knickers showing. It is just horrible and there really is no excuse for it. Don't bother with tit tape, or whatever they call it, which you see in some high-street stores: go to a proper wig shop and get the real stuff as it's much tougher and nothing will go anywhere when you've got that on. Word of warning, though: be careful when you take it off that you don't rip a nipple off too, as it really is very strong!

When choosing a dress, keep in mind how it will look under certain lights. I recently made myself a dress, long and flesh-coloured, but when I wore it in front of my mirror with the light behind me, I realized it was totally see-through! So that one went back in the closet. I'd learned my lesson before about that: once I went out in a summer dress and the next day it was all over the tabloids – 'Posh Nips Out'. It was horrible as I'm a bit prudish about things like that: a bit of bra strap showing in the Dolce kind of way, OK; the whole deal, no.

you wear a bra is to make sure you have toupee tape to keep everything in place

One thing I personally don't like is too much heavy beading and too many jewels on a dress. It can look tacky, weigh the dress down and make it very expensive all at the same time. In vintage shops you can find fabulous flapper dresses made out of beads that make the dress hang down very elegantly. But when lots of beads are simply placed on top of the fabric they just give the dress unnecessary added bulk.

As I've said before, it's almost always best to avoid fussy or challenging outfits, and when going to big parties it is triply important to avoid anything that has the potential to look a total disaster in photos, especially as these are the places where everyone is taking pictures. You'll be stuck with those party snaps for ever. It's a funny thing but the two situations when people often dress the worst are also the times when they get photographed

Dresses

It's best to go for something really simple or a shape that has been around for ages and is timeless. That's why I love clothes that look as if they're almost from a different era, like VIVIENNE WESTWOOD's or ALEXANDER McQUEEN's dresses.

the most – holidays and big parties. So just bear that in mind when you're packing and when you're looking in your closet, getting ready for a night out.

Speaking of photos, a lot of people often get nervous about posing for snapshots at parties, and who can blame them? I still feel nervous when I'm walking down the red carpet and I see all the cameras pointing at me. Elizabeth Hurley told me her posing trick is to stand with one leg sticking out and then pout her lips on the exhale. That might work for her but I could never quite get the hang of this. I don't really have a red-carpet pose, I just want to get from one end to the other and into wherever I'm going.

If you're going to buy a dress for a big party, be careful not to get one that's too obviously in fashion at the moment because party dresses can be expensive and you'll have spent a lot of money on something you can wear only a few times before it dates. It's best to go for something really simple or a shape that has been around for ages and is timeless. That's why I love clothes that look as if they're almost from a different era, like Vivienne Westwood's or Alexander McQueen's dresses. Both of these designers often use historical references, from the French seventeenth-century aristocracy to Hitchcock films. Ironically, these are the styles that really don't date as they've been around and loved for so long that they are now bona fide classics.

Don't get swayed by a label. The most important thing is how the dress looks, because that's what people will see, not the label! Nothing shows up your less-than-perfect features more quickly than just blindly following a trend or designer name.

After all, when you see women whose outfits are based on how many labels they can wear at the same time – in other words, they look like they've just gone into a department store, covered in superglue, rolled around the floor and come out with as much stuck to their bodies as possible, whether it suits them or not – that is most definitely not fashionable.

But just because you're concentrating on what styles suit you best, this does not mean you should limit yourself to a few set looks simply out of habit. I recently went to dinner at Valentino's house and I wore a big ruffly party dress that was a totally different look from my usual style. But it appealed to me, somehow, despite all the frilliness, so I decided to take a risk, and it really worked and it's now one of my favourite party dresses. It's very easy to get stuck in a style rut but you sometimes

When you see women whose outfits are based on how many labels they can wear at the same time — in other words, they look like they've just gone into a department store, covered in superglue, rolled around the floor and come out with as much stuck to their bodies as possible, whether it suits them or not — that is most definitely not fashionable

have to force yourself to not put your blinkers on and to keep looking around. Personal shoppers in department stores can often help with that, and if you're home all day with the kids you can easily just flick through some magazines for inspiration. Friends can help in that respect too, and I get a lot of fashion inspiration just from looking at other people on the street. Suddenly, you'll see someone wearing something unexpected and looking totally amazing, and you'll wonder why you never thought of it yourself. Some high-street stores are now offering a personal shopping service.

Looking at celebrities in magazines can also give you ideas as they will often get the latest styles and looks before they hit the shops, thanks to stylists and designers lending them pieces from the latest collections. So you can see months in advance what shoes work best with what dresses, and so on, and you can start looking through your wardrobe to see which pieces you have already. It's also a good idea to concentrate on celebrities who bear the most resemblance to you, even if it's just skin tone, hair colour or body shape, to get a better idea of what would look best on you. But, if you do get inspired by a celebrity's outfit, the key thing to bear in mind is, again, that you have to give the look your own individual twist. If you saw a particular photo of that celebrity in that magazine, chances are other people will have done too — and also, just because they looked good in that outfit, there is no

Wearing something quite masculine is often really sexy in a Patti Smith way, and can still cause as much of an impact as it did back in 1966

guarantee that you will, as we've already discussed in regard to taking inspiration from Kate Moss. By all means take tips from magazines and celebrities, but have the confidence to do your own take on the outfit and wear something that shows your individual touch. Treat these celebrity photos as a springboard from which you can get inspiration – but then go a bit further with them.

One of my favourite things to do in London is just to drive around and look at what people on the street are wearing because, honestly, no other city can provide as much fashion inspiration as London. The trick is to have the confidence to try variations of these outfits for yourself and then find ways to make them individual to you, such as adding your favourite accessories. But don't forget to be honest with yourself if it's just not working. That's when it's crucial to have someone you know who's honest, who will tell you the truth and won't let you go out looking like a total disaster.

Another thing you mustn't get distracted by is sizing. Almost every woman I know finds this the difficult part of shopping, and it is gutting to try on a dress in your usual size only to find it doesn't fit. But we've talked about this already with regard to trousers. The thing you have to remember is that there is no real standardization when it comes to sizing, so you could be a 14 in one shop and a 10 in another – really, those little numbers mean nothing. All that matters is finding a dress that fits well; numbers are literally meaningless.

Of course, you don't have to wear a dress to parties. Wearing something quite masculine is often really sexy in a Patti Smith way, and can still cause as much of an impact as it did back in 1966 when Yves Saint Laurent first showed this look with his famous Le Smoking, a stylishly louche tuxedo for women. I recently gave this look a go and wore a trouser suit by Jaeger, a label I'd never tried before, and it worked because the suit was very clearly a great cut, with fantastic trousers that were narrow around the legs and had a defined waist. I then tied a thick piece of fat fabric which acted like a cummerbund around the white shirt underneath the jacket, to emphasize the curves and make it sexy but still masculine and sharp. It's the same with low-slung boyish trousers and mannish jackets: always make sure they're cut for your shape, whatever that is, or you could potentially look shapeless as opposed to sexily subversive. Viktor & Rolf make very sharp and sexy trouser suits that look fantastic.

IF YOU'RE WEARING A FULL OR DECORATED SKIRT, KEEP YOUR TOP SIMPLE, LIKE THE TULLE SKIRT/TIGHT TOP COMBO THAT I LOVE SO MUCH

If you find dresses a little overwhelming but still want to go for a feminine look, there are so many pretty skirts out there, such as ones trimmed with beads or delicate piping. Elspeth Gibson does really beautiful ones, if you're looking to spend some serious money; Eley Kishimoto, Nanette Lepore and Marc by Marc Jacobs do cute ones and, on the high street, there's always a huge number to choose from. But, as I said earlier, if you're wearing a full or decorated skirt, keep your top simple, like the tulle skirt/tight top combo that I love so much.

If you're going to the party with your boyfriend or partner, you should think about what the other person is wearing and, no, I'm not about to tell you to wear matching leather outfits. But you should check that the two of you won't clash, and if my husband was going to wear trainers to a party then I probably wouldn't wear a full-length dress. Anyway, it's fun to get ready with your partner, helping each other pick out what to wear, getting their opinion about your outfit. After all, they're the one who you want to look nicest for, and you can also gently steer them away from choosing anything awful that would just embarrass you. You see? Fun but also practical.

Accessories are where you can really go to town with your party outfit if you've

Handbag by Roberto Cavalli

Accessories are where you can really go to town with your party outfit if you've played it safe with the dress

played it safe with the dress. And, best of all, it's the high street that often supplies the most fabulous finishing touches. I'm not much of a one for earrings but I do like big hoops and you can get those from pretty much any high-street or department store, though I think Agatha makes the best. Topshop earrings are fun and always bang on with the latest trend. Warehouse often has pretty little chain-metal clutch bags. I love wearing gloves, either demi ones that cut across the knuckle, or full-on opera versions, and you can usually get those from Accessorize, H&M or Claire's Accessories. Monsoon often has pretty vintage-style pieces – clutch bags studded with pearls or fans with feathers. Go to specialist Chinese shops – the best are, unsurprisingly, in London's Chinatown – for more authentic fans, and you can also get lovely painted-wood jewellery. Vintage shops always have fantastic party pieces, particularly Patricia Field in New York and Virginia in London, as do high-street stores, as we talked about in the accessories section.

I was never one of those little girls who sat around and dreamed about her wedding day and it wasn't until I met

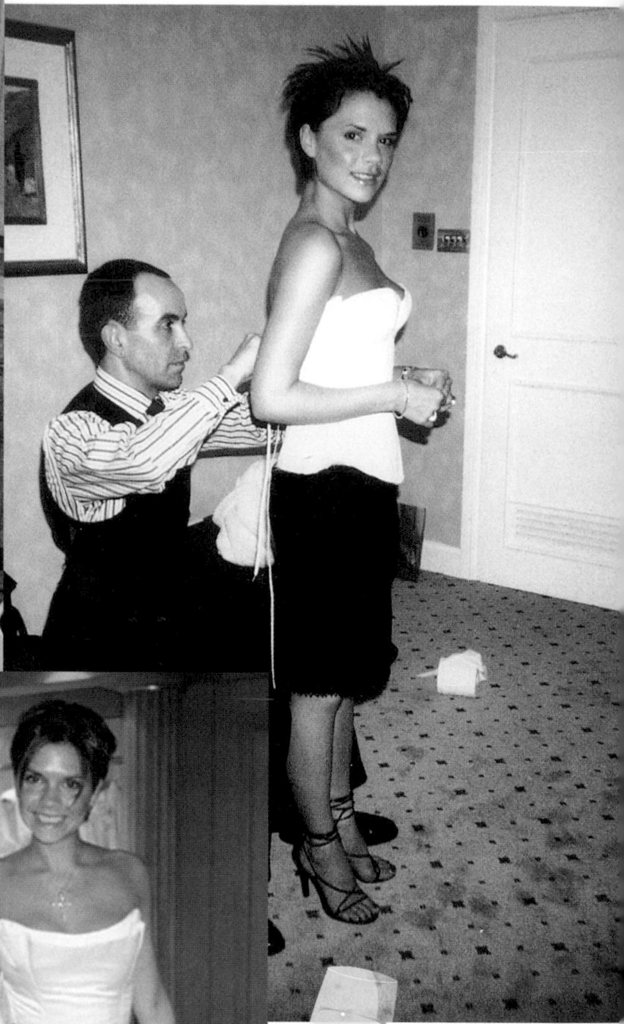

*F*ittings for
the happiest
day of my life

David that I thought I'd want to get married at all. But once I decided to, I had a pretty good idea how I wanted the wedding to look. My taste, as you can probably tell by now, tends to lean towards the classical side so I wanted a clean, simple gown and I'm so pleased I went for that because I still love the dress, after all these years.

My dress was made by Vera Wang, who's famous for making really timeless, elegant wedding dresses, and the corset was made by a man called Mr Pearl. Now, he really is a bit of a character. He wears a corset himself all the time, even to bed, because he is so focused on maintaining his 18-inch waist. So he wears it literally day and night, which is true dedication to one's figure. But his corsets do honestly give you that womanly, 50s silhouette that I love, and it felt so sexy having that on my wedding day.

Flowers can be tough as they're so expensive. So to make things less complicated, and possibly even cheaper, I recommend going with a theme. At our wedding, I wanted to stick with the colour theme of our house, which is deep purple, red and green, particularly as I think strong colours give a really good dramatic effect. Alternatively, all white flowers at a wedding always look lovely but, for heaven's sake, don't include carnations – they are far too petrol station for your wedding day. Or you can skip flowers altogether and go for a more rustic theme with leaves, moss and twigs, especially if you're having an autumn wedding. Fruit can also look lovely – we had piles of apples by our wedding cake and they looked beautiful. So you see, you don't have to spend a fortune and cover everywhere with orchids.

Bridesmaids' outfits are tough because it's tempting to skimp on them after having spent so much on your own. But you're doing yourself no favours because it's your wedding so surely you should try to make it look as nice as possible.

I wanted my sister up there with me, but she said she was too old to be a bridesmaid. So I bribed her with a Chloe dress and we compromised with matron of honour. I ended up having younger bridesmaids – my two nieces – and got their outfits from Angels, a costumier in London. The point is, think outside the box when it comes to dresses for the bridesmaids and matron of honour because people tend to automatically go for that funny, frumpy style when you really don't have to. If you do have older bridesmaids a good tip is to get pretty party dresses that they can wear after the wedding, like I did with Louise and the Chloe dress. It's just a thoughtful gesture to them.

In terms of other special occasions, if you're going out for a romantic meal, all the

Miss Victoria Adams Project

Original illustrations of ideas for Victoria's wedding shoes designed exclusively for her by Manolo Blahnik

'*She's a lovely lady and when I met her, I was amazed at how much better she looks in real life than she does in pictures. And she moves so beautifully. She's petite and very, very charming*'

MANOLO BLAHNIK

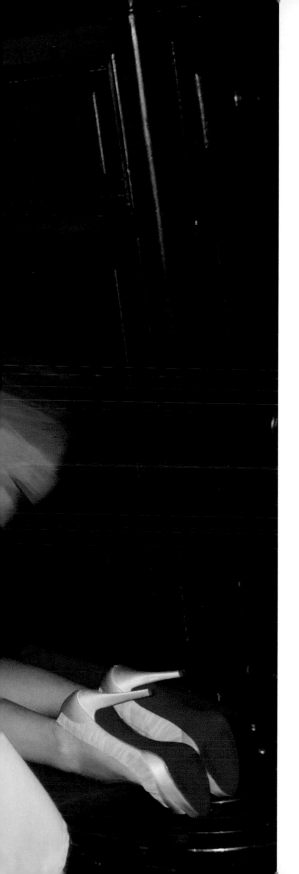

YOU CAN MAKE ANYTHING INTO A SPECIAL OCCASION AND DRESS UP FOR IT

rules I mentioned earlier about date outfits apply:
show off your good features, but keep it modest.
You can make anything into a special occasion
and dress up for it. Iconic fashion stylist, Isabella
Blow, is my absolute heroine on that front. She
once came with us to a football game in
Manchester wearing a fabulous pencil skirt,
fishnet tights, a really tight leather jacket, major
high heels and a Philip Treacy hat that had a big
cut-out photo of David on it – with a real
diamond in his ear. At Manchester United! Can
you imagine? She did look fantastic but when she
walked in, well, it was definitely a bit more
dressed up than the usual style at Old Trafford!

WHERE TO SHOP

1. PARTY DRESSES

Valentino, Versace, Alexander McQueen, Vivienne Westwood, Roberto Cavalli, Marc by Marc Jacobs, Elie Saab, Reiss, Topshop, Principles

2. SMART TROUSER SUITS

Dolce & Gabbana, Gucci, Jaeger, Reiss, Karen Millen

3. SKIRTS *Prada, Elspeth Gibson, Eley Kishimoto, Nanette Lepore, Marc by Marc Jacobs, Topshop, Principles*

4. PARTY ACCESSORIES *Christian Dior, Gucci, Dolce & Gabbana, Roberto Cavalli, Agatha, Warehouse, H&M, Claire's Accessories, Monsoon, Mikey, Marks & Spencer, Topshop, oriental stores*

Vacations

Bayswater bag by MULBERRY;
Bikini and flip-flops by TOPSHOP

PACKING REALLY IS ONE OF THE WORST THINGS ABOUT HOLIDAYS. I JUST HATE CHOOSING WHAT TO TAKE AND WHAT TO LEAVE OUT. SO I TAKE EVERYTHING!

I'VE TRIED TO GET BETTER ABOUT THIS, though, because a few years ago I learned a harsh lesson. Yes, it was that ultimate holiday nightmare – my cases were stolen. And the worst thing was, I had packed everything in them, and I mean EVERYTHING. Like, there was this fantastic little Zara vest that I'd bought five years previously. As all girls know, it's not always the most valuable things that are irreplaceable. There are still times when I'm standing in front of my closet, deciding what to wear that day and thinking, 'Oh, yes, I'll wear those shoes with that dress' – and then I'll remember that those shoes are long gone.

Let's start with the basics. Don't bother with flashy designer luggage. There is a good chance it could get stolen as it attracts attention. Instead, just get plain black cases. I really like the Tumi range, which is expensive but is low key and high quality, the two things you want from your cases. I've also heard very good things about Marks & Spencer luggage. Wheelie luggage is a total godsend especially if, like me, you take a lot of stuff on holiday, as you can just pull your bag around instead of carrying it and ending up with one arm longer than the other. Sometimes you can slip your wheelie bag onto the plane with you instead of having to check it in and wait

Wheelie luggage is a total godsend especially if, like me, you take a lot of stuff on holiday

ages hanging about the carousel at the other end. If you're just going for a weekend all you need is a hold-all, and you can get good hardy leather ones from second-hand markets all over the place. One of the best countries for this is Morocco, so if you ever go to Marrakech make sure you go to the leather-goods stall in the main souk as they make some of the best – and cheapest – leather bags in the world. And, as I said earlier, I'm lucky enough to have leather of fantastic quality right on my doorstep here in Spain, where it is a major national industry.

Personally, I won't go anywhere without my hair straighteners, my Mason Pearson hairbrush, my rollers and hairpins, a small make-up bag, toothbrush and toothpaste, Elizabeth Arden 8 Hour Cream and eye cream. That's pretty much the essentials. If I'm going for a week, I'll bring three pairs of jeans – in other words, a different pair for every other day – because they really are my staple, as you know. Then I try to stick to the formula of bringing something casual (plain T-shirts), something a bit more rock 'n' roll (vintage T-shirts and minidresses or miniskirts), something classic (nice V-necks, a pencil skirt and a plain dress) and then something a bit more out there for some fun. For example, a recent 'out there' outfit was a pair of leather chaps that I took to LA last year, which Dean and Dan Caton from DSquared[2] kindly gave me. Maybe they were a little too different for some people but I loved them and had a lot of fun with them, and that's what really matters. Oh, yes, and always bring a dressy outfit as you just never know where your holiday might take you.

Also, pack some little slipper bags as they are so useful for putting your dirty knickers and socks in on the way back. It's just good sense to separate them out and secure them properly. I once saw some poor woman at an airport whose suitcase fell open on the carousel and she had to go scurrying around, chasing after all her dirty knickers on the conveyor belt, in front of everyone! Can you imagine?

In your carry-on bag, I recommend bringing a tracksuit you can change into if it's a long-haul journey; Johnson's baby wipes to take your make-up off; a good, heavy moisturizer; eye cream; lip balm; herbal sleeping pills; Chantecaille's Rose Water or Evian Spritz to help refresh and hydrate your face and get rid of that awful plane smell; some music and a pile of magazines and books you've been saving up. That can pretty much get you through any flight, I find. Get a good-sized carry-on bag that you can fit all of this into instead of relying on multiple handbags. Everyone picks up

Make-up bag by Paul & Joe

Agent
Provocateur

Topshop

water, magazines and so on at the airport, so you want to be able to fit as many extra last-minute purchases in your hand luggage as possible, otherwise you'll find yourself carrying about four different bags.

I'm much worse at packing for beach holidays than for skiing ones simply because I always end up bringing so much stuff that I never wear. For some reason, I always bring lots of dressy tops and trousers but, of course, I mainly wear T-shirts and cut-off shorts on beach holidays.

Agent Provocateur

Pistol Panties

A bikini wax is a completely crucial pre-holiday treatment. There is nothing worse than seeing someone throwing their legs around on the beach and, well, let us say no more. I also recommend getting your legs properly waxed as otherwise you'll be shaving every other day, which is not only not exactly glamorous and can also give you those horrible red bumps. Waxing, however, makes your legs look smooth and shiny. There are so many good places around now: Vaishaly and Heidi Klein in London and the Lowry Hotel's spa in Manchester. My favourite place is Strip in

FOR SUNBATHING,
I PREFER BIKINIS TO
ONE-PIECES SIMPLY
BECAUSE YOU GET
LESS TAN MARKS

London. It is such a pretty little shop and salon where they do the most brilliant waxes and sell beautiful lingerie, and the fact that it is owned by my best friend is purely coincidence...

For sunbathing, I prefer bikinis to one-pieces simply because you get less tan marks, and bikinis generally give a better shape. Whatever your shape and preference, you can find fantastic ones on the high street, with Topshop and H&M making some of the best. Sportswear brands, particularly Adidas, can do good ones too, in nice colours.

I do love designer swimsuits but you have to be careful not to get one cut in odd shapes or with funny cut-outs on the side, which will just give you comedy tan marks. It takes a very special kind of woman to carry off having brown diamond-shaped marks going down the left side of her ribcage.

Very cute 50s-pin-up bikinis with boy-shorts or pretty little skirts attached to the bottoms are so flirty and a million times sexier than some of the shocking swimming costumes you see some women wearing. The worst are those really high cut, 80s-style swimsuits. What is the point of those? They just make you look like you're wearing a wrestler's outfit. Um, very sexy, I don't think so... G-string bikinis? Totally not necessary. The weirdest one, though, I think, is when women deliberately wear those triangle bikinis that are too small for them so that half of their boobs are hanging out underneath. How anyone can think that looks sexy is beyond me.

If you're also a bikini girl, get ones that tie at the

Very cute 50s-pin-up bikinis with boy-shorts or pretty little skirts attached to the bottoms are so flirty and a million times sexier than some of the shocking swimming costumes you see some women wearing

175 **Vacations**

sides. That way, you can adjust them so they don't dig into your hips when you sit down – and, of course, they're sexier. Topshop, in particular, and H&M do great string bikinis every summer in really cute colours and patterns and you can get some great ones in big department stores in America. Polo Ralph Lauren, for example, makes really fun ones. In terms of colour, the best thing to do is to try to match your skin tone, so if you've got olive skin, like me, brown is a good bet and, once you're tanned, bright orange, yellow or even classy black always look good.

As for what else to wear around the pool, well, I don't want to disillusion anybody but I generally opt for just some flip-flops, usually from Topshop, and suncream. Weirdly, I read somewhere recently that I wore high heels even when I go swimming. Now come on – why would anyone do that to Manolo Blahnik? It would be just criminal.

I love to wear more natural jewellery on holiday – an anklet or bracelet made of shells or pieces of aquamarine. Accessorize is brilliant for that kind of stuff and they usually have very prettily decorated flip-flops. I also really love body jewellery and will sometimes wear a little tummy chain.

There's no need to feel dull on the beach: Topshop has a fantastic beach range with lots of really cool towels and bits and bobs. Gap has started doing oversized floppy sun hats and decorated beach sandals. Kate Spade's beach range is really terrific: simple and classic beach bags and towels that are expensive but last for ages. Heidi Klein in London has some of the most amazing, if quite expensive, pieces for beach holidays, from suits to hats to bracelets, which definitely prove that you don't have to be boring on the beach. The key is to look nice but not to overdo it.

I'm not all that keen on women in long sarongs, although I know loads of people swear by them. Maybe just a little one when you're wearing a bikini, but keep the pattern simple as otherwise it can overwhelm you, not to mention any onlookers. Same story for kaftans, which can look very 70s in a good way. But, equally, they can make people look like they're wearing monks' habits. If you feel too self-conscious to be parading about in your bikini just slip on a little cotton summer dress or a pair of denim shorts – far cooler and prettier and you won't look like a monk in a designer pattern.

For bags, it's best to have a waterproof one – obvious, really! Don't load up on too much stuff as it's easy for things to be ruined or even stolen on the beach, so just take the bare minimum.

I try to get a tan on my body and leave my face lighter, which means my beach formula is sunblock on the face and a high-factor suntan lotion on the body

To get a good colour on holiday, exfoliate beforehand as this will ensure you get the best colour. Yes, it does mean that you'll look like a pasty ghost for your first few days of holiday but the end results will compensate. My favourite scrubs are both from Origins – Never A Dull Moment for my face and Paradise Found for my body, both of which I rely on for my pre-holiday prep. Of course, though, you have to be very careful when you tan and make sure you get a good sunscreen with a high SPF. No one wants to end up looking like one of those old ladies with a face like a Louis Vuitton handbag. In fact, I tend to try to get a tan on my body and leave my face lighter, which means my beach formula is sunblock on the face and a high-factor suntan lotion on the body. Having a tan on your face also means that you have to change your usual make-up palette, which is a total pain. Who can be bothered with that on holiday? So, given all the important health issues, be extra careful about covering yourself in sunscreen every time you go out.

You have to look after your hair particularly carefully on beach holidays as the sun and salty sea are complete killers and, if you don't treat it well, you'll look like a giant Brillo pad, and everyone will have their holiday snaps for proof and potential future blackmail. Remember that episode of *Friends* when they all went to Barbados and Monica's hair went totally mental in the heat? And you thought TV wasn't educational. So, first of all, always wear a hat to protect your hair from the sun: this is doubly important if you have any colour or chemicals in your hair. As I mentioned earlier, I really love wearing cowboy hats on the beach as they're a little bit different from all the floppy straw satellites you usually see yet they still provide good shade for your face and neck. Giving your hair special treatments every two days or so, such as Aussie 3 Minute Miracle treatment or Louise Galvin Sacred Locks, for instance, will help to remoisturize it.

Skiing holidays are, of course, a complete nightmare to pack for as you have to bring so much heavy stuff. My main problem is that I find it tricky to get any decent ski clothes: they tend to be hugely bulky or skin-tight salopettes. My only advice is to get professional ski clothes, like North Face, because at least then you'll be sure that the clothes are warm and look great. Otherwise, the rest of your necessities are a good sunblock, a fabulous pair of sunglasses (I'm really not into the goggle look) and a warm, thick headband to protect your ears and keep your hair from flying about and blinding you. I don't tend to wear a hat, mainly because I never ski when it's really cold so it's just not necessary. If I did, though, I don't think I could get away with one of those bobble hats. Earmuffs can be fun but, personally, it's not a look for me.

The one item you should definitely spend some money on is a pair of gloves as you want to make sure you get a really good pair that are lined and waterproof. It is just dreadful skiing with cold hands so, for heaven's sake, never ski with fingerless gloves.

You can have some fun with your après-ski look. My favourite outfit for that is a fitted jumper or hooded top, a trusted pair of jeans and some moon boots (Marc Jacobs makes great ones) as they are so warm and comforting after a day on the slopes. Another rule is no winter holiday-themed clothes, so definitely no Bridget Jones-style snowflake jumpers if you're over the age of six. My other best beloved après-ski outfit is a sleeveless thick jumper dress which is cosy but doesn't add bulk. Pair it all with a good pair of boots and you're set up nicely for an evening in the chalet with fondue and a glass of Glühwein.

WHAT TO PACK

1. BEACH *miniskirts, jeans, shorts, summer cotton dresses, sunglasses, a wrap dress, flip-flops, sandals, string bikinis, towel, beach bag, suncream and sunblock, hair treatments*

2. SKI *sunglasses, hairband, thick warm gloves, skisuit, waterproof boots, hooded tops, long-sleeved tops and jumpers, jeans, warm socks, jumper dresses*

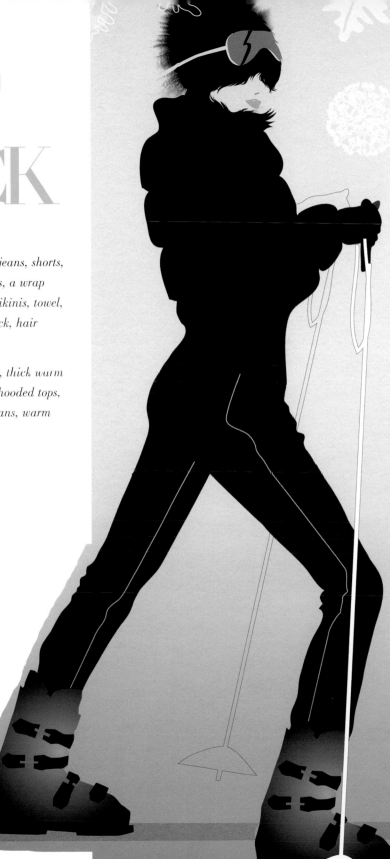

Winter

Boot by GUCCI, vintage fake fur scarf from a selection
at RADIO DAYS, gloves by CAROLINA HERRERA

PEOPLE OFTEN THINK WINTER IS ABOUT BUNDLING UP AND FEELING FRUMPY AND MISERABLE. BUT IT CAN BE EASIER TO LOOK STYLISH IN COLD WEATHER THAN WHEN IT'S WARM.

PEOPLE OFTEN JUST WILT IN THE HEAT AND GET STUCK IN THE OLD VEST-AND-SHORTS RUT, WHICH IS FINE, BUT NOT A VERY SOPHISTICATED LOOK. In autumn and winter I'll wear a coat, nice shoes and well-fitting trousers, and, with a cool handbag, you can't get more sophisticated than that. It's easy to panic about buying a coat because in all likelihood that's the winter item you'll spend the most money on and so you'll want to invest in a proper one that will keep you warm for years and won't look dated. So it's best to go with a classic coat as opposed to something that's too fashionable that season. What you want instead is a shape that's proven to be timeless and that you can wear with jeans and dresses.

Trench coats definitely fulfil those criteria. Obviously, the original and the best are by Burberry, but these are very expensive. You can occasionally find old second-hand Burberry trenches at markets, particularly Portobello, or, if you're lucky, at charity shops. However, since the whole trench trend started up again the high street

> *Victoria has such a strong personal love of fashion and clothes. She is able to successfully balance her hectic work, travel and family, with a real individual style*

CHRISTOPHER BAILEY
CREATIVE DIRECTOR, BURBERRY

has been doing good versions, especially the mini trench, which is easier to wear. They've even done trench-style jackets that are just great with jeans in the late autumn and early spring. You can get trenches in the traditional khaki or off-white, almost bone-coloured, tone, and both are good, though obviously the off-white one is going to be harder to keep clean. A red trench is great if you're going for a bit of a siren look and a black one will make any outfit look pulled together and elegant. Back to Burberry, the Creative Director, Christopher Bailey, has cleverly made the trench a little more dressy in Burberry's high fashion line, Burberry Prorsum (which is Latin for 'forward'), by offering them in gorgeous metallic fabrics, such as shimmery silver. They are absolutely beautiful but, as you'd expect, are expensive. There are some smart trenches around by small cult labels. 3.1 Phillip Lim, which you can find in boutiques like Matches SPY and on www.net-a-porter.com, has made some beautiful ones.

Properly lined leather jackets also work and they almost always look better the older they get. You often find them in vintage shops and second-hand markets like

Trench

Trench coats fulfil every criteria. The original and the best are by Burberry London

Burberry London

Classic

Hobbs

Hobbs has a sweet and pretty selection of smart classic coats

All Saints

Make sure that the coat is warm. No matter how beautiful it is, you just won't wear it if it's not doing its primary job

Reiss

If you want to get a trendy winter coat, you can buy great ones off the high street at shops like Reiss and that way you won't have spent too much money when the look has moved on

High Street

Trench coats can often be shapeless so check that yours is properly cut along

Covent Garden. Rick Owens makes some of the sexiest ones, but they are expensive. Balenciaga is another high-end label that does incredibly sexy leather jackets, which I always lust after. But then, Christobal Balenciaga was Spanish so maybe I'm biased!

For smart, classic coats, Hobbs has a sweet and very pretty selection every autumn, like wool ones with scalloped edges or long black ones with a bit of skirting on the bottom half to keep them looking feminine – a trick Burberry Prorsum and Marks & Spencer use too. Gap, Principles and Oasis have started to do good tweed ones and H&M's colourful tweed coats are famously good.

For a more expensive investment, Miu Miu, Sara Berman, Philosophy di Alberta Ferretti, Cavalli, Versace and Betty Jackson make absolutely beautiful coats but, like I said, they are much more expensive.

If you want to get a trendy winter coat, you can buy great ones off the high street and that way you won't have spent too much money when the look has moved on.

Don't forget about practicalities, either: I do love how capes look but, I have to be honest, they are not the most practical when you're running about with the kids all day, and I speak from experience on that one. Last winter, I bought a really beautiful biscuit-coloured cape by the Italian designer Ana Molinari, which I love and it looks great and stylish, but it isn't very practical in my day-to-day life. Also, always make sure that the coat is warm. No matter how beautiful it is, you just won't wear it if it's not doing its primary job.

Certain coats can often be shapeless so check that yours is properly cut along the torso, otherwise you can look a little lumpen. It should nip in around the waist, either in

the torso . . . it should nip in around the waist and have a belt you can tie

the way it is cut at the back or from having a belt that you can tie at the front or the back. This is why I like cropped jackets – although they are more autumnal and not very suitable for winter – because they show off your shape in a way that most coats and jackets don't. Designers like Marni, Cavalli and Dolce & Gabbana started doing these first but the beloved high steet has picked up on them and there are some really good versions around.

Be careful when you're buying denim jackets as some can be really shapeless. Abercrombie & Fitch do great ones that nip in at the waist, as does Warehouse,

Leather gloves are always the way to go and you can get some really beautifully coloured ones from traditional places like Dents

giving them a more feminine look.

Winter footwear can be tricky too. I admit, I do wear open-toed sandals in the winter. However, I live in a warm country where it hardly ever rains. But this is so not a good idea if you live in a wet country. I haven't really got into the tights with open-toed shoes look that is very popular now, particularly in England. It's just more sensible, and more classic, to wear pointy or round-toed shoes or boots instead during the winter. Remember to make sure your trousers break just on the tips of the shoes to elongate your limbs.

But this is not to say that you can't have a bit of fun with your winter accessories. Gloves, for example, can really style up an outfit: a few years ago I bought a pair of really fun demi gloves with fake-fur trim from Vivienne Westwood and they still look amazing.

Leather gloves are always the way to go and you can get some really beautifully coloured ones from traditional places like Dents, which make jewel-coloured ones in soft, thin leather. Gucci does great ones too, which isn't all that surprising as the label has always specialized in leather, and the same for Hermès, and Carolina Herrera makes very pretty and feminine ones. At the other end of the spectrum, my sister bought me some amazing olive-green ones from H&M a while ago, made from the most beautiful leather.

Long chunky scarves look really beautiful and I recommend Louis Vuitton and Burberry. You can get them all over the high street, especially from New Look and Topshop. Very Ali MacGraw in *Love Story* I think, tragic ending aside, of course.

Gloves by H&M

WHERE TO SHOP

1. TRENCH COATS
Burberry, second-hand markets, 3.1 Phillip Lim, Gap, Topshop

2. LEATHER JACKETS
Dolce & Gabbana, Gucci, Balenciaga, second-hand markets

3. CLASSIC COATS
Versace, Balenciaga, Dolce & Gabbana, Roberto Cavalli, Miu Miu at www.net-a-porter.com, Philosophy di Alberta Ferretti, Sara Berman, Betty Jackson, Reiss, Hobbs, Gap, H&M, Marks and Spencer, Principles, Oasis

4. TRENDY COATS
Roberto Cavalli, Balenciaga, Topshop, H&M

5. CROPPED JACKETS
Marni, Roberto Cavalli, Dolce & Gabbana, Topshop, Gap, Urban Outfitters

6. DENIM JACKETS
Abercrombie & Fitch, Warehouse, Levi's

7. GLOVES *Vivienne Westwood, Gucci, Hermès, Carolina Herrera, Dents, H&M*

8. SCARVES *Louis Vuitton, Burberry, New Look, Topshop, H&M*

winter

195

Special
Occasions

Camel classic quilted bag and faux
pearl belt by CHANEL; black gift box
by WWW.NET-A-PORTER.COM;
orange gift box by HERMES;
yellow gift box by FENDI

THE FIRST THING I WILL SAY ABOUT HOLIDAY DRESSING IS TO GET ALL IMAGES OF REINDEER JUMPERS OUT OF YOUR HEAD.

ONLY CHILDREN SHOULD WEAR CLOTHES SPECIFIC TO AN OCCASION – HALLOWE'EN OR CHRISTMAS, SAY. I love putting the boys in Christmas pyjamas, and that kind of thing. However, for adults, dressing at Christmas is about being comfortable but also looking decent, as chances are you'll all be taking photos of one another and you really don't want photographs of you in a reindeer jumper to sit in your living room for the rest of your life. If it's just us, I'll often simply wear my pyjamas and a dressing gown and then brush my hair up into a ponytail. If we have family over for a traditional Christmas dinner I'll put on a nice pair of trousers and a good shirt. I'm certainly not going to be tottering about the house all day in some uncomfortable get-up. David will wear a nice shirt and simple trousers, and I'll put the kids in jumpers and corduroy trousers, so hopefully we'll all look smart yet easy and relaxed. Basically, we tend to go down the traditional route.

Buying fashion presents for Christmas is a highly risky affair but there are some things that are always going to be winners, even if the gift is for the toughest sort of fashion snob who seems to have everything. Diptyque candles are forever popular, come in a huge range of gorgeous fragrances and they will always be appreciated by a stylish recipient. Diptyque also now sells a selection of smaller candles. The White Company has really nice candles too, and Jo Malone's range is rightly a classic. She

also does very pretty scents and lovely room fragrances, particularly the Pine & Eucalyptus, which instantly makes any room smell like Christmas, whatever the time of year. David and I also both love the scented candles from Hotel Costes in Paris; they have a really strong, sexy smell and always make us feel like we're in that gorgeous city, even if we're just playing with the kids in the kitchen. Liberty's in London has a fantastic selection of really unusual candles, including ranges from Comme des Garçons to Slatkin. Excitingly, my favourite shoe designer – yes, Manolo Blahnik – has started making candles, so if you can't quite stretch to a pair of Manolo stilettos, at least you can get some beautiful-smelling scents! There are plenty of the cheaper range of scented candles around but these tend not to last very long because they contain relatively little of the oil that gives the candle its smell. So if you can buy a more expensive one, you'll find you burn it for less time and it therefore lasts an age.

Pretty things from Smythson, such as plain notecards or funny little notebooks – you can get cute doll-sized ones that aren't too expensive – always look wonderful and they giftwrap things so beautifully there. Cath Kidston also does really pretty, vintage-looking things such as gorgeous mugs and little bags.

I do think it's a bit of a risk to buy actual clothes for your girlfriends unless you know for sure beforehand that they like the item and that you've bought it in the right size. Yes, of course, you can always include the receipt so they can return it, but it is a bit of a pain for the person to have to go back to the shop. Little

Bath products in general are a good idea as surely everybody loves

accessories are generally safer bets, such as small, pretty handbags, clutch bags, or even bits of jewellery or pretty compact mirrors. Teeny little designer things that have the designer's name or logo on them are always cute, such as tiny Prada key rings or Miu Miu brooches. The Marc by Marc Jacobs store in New York is the best place in the world for this. There, you can find Marc Jacobs colouring pencils, pretty plastic compacts, animal-shaped pencil sharpeners and sweet little pens, all for under $20. So if you ever go to New York, go straight there and stock up because you can give those as presents for years. In the UK, little boutiques such as Matches and Press in London stock similar, if a little more expensive, designer knick-knacks, for example tiny Marc

Jacobs purses and small Missoni head scarves. Vintage shops and special boutiques like Coco Ribbon are also great for things like beautiful feathered fans and lacy parasols.

Giving beauty products and make-up can be equally tricky but there are some things that any girl would love. Nars Body Glow and MAC's Strobe Lotion are

having a pampering bath

both fabulous, giving a subtle sheen to your skin, and they work brilliantly on bare legs and arms in the summer. The Laura Mercier body and bath range is divine: the Almond Coconut Milk Scrub makes you smell absolutely delicious, and the Crème Brûlée Honey Bath is the most soothing thing in the world after a long day. It even comes with a cute

laura mercier body and bath

almond coconut milk honey bath

little honey dipper to help you scoop the product into the bath, which just makes it even more fun. Geri first introduced me to these products and she gave me a whole basketful after I had Cruz; it was the perfect post-birth present.

Bath products in general are a good idea as surely everybody loves having a pampering bath; or just a pot of really gorgeous moisturizer! Anyway, a boxed set of Origins' A Perfect World range is fantastic, and Miller Harris does some great shower gels in really prettily decorated packaging – they are lovely to see first thing in the morning.

Nice little home-ware pieces are good too. I am totally addicted to Zara Home for this as they have some really great things: attractively decorated picture frames, unique-looking notebooks and really nice glasses and goblets – all at Zara-sized prices. I totally rely on it out here in Spain. Just bear in mind the style of the recipient's home, and not yours! Also, just getting someone basics is often a good idea simply because you'll know they'll use them. My mum always buys me the basic essentials. For my birthday last year, for example, she got me a Marks & Spencer picture frame and some Primark knickers.

For someone really special, buying them a professional facial or massage is a real treat. I hear Jo Malone gives some of the best facials, and the Elemis spa in London has to be one of the most amazing inner-city spas in the world. You enter through this little door on a cobbled street and it's like you're in some mysterious Moroccan temple; and the treatments themselves are incredible. Sticking with London, Harrods offers wonderful treatments, especially its particularly luxurious Crème de la Mer facial. Dermalogica facials are super-effective and you can find your nearest branch at www.dermalogica.co.uk. Bliss spa in London and New York is so white and clean you feel refreshed before you've even had anything done to you. For a cheaper but still good facial, The Green Room uses entirely The Body Shop products and has branches all over London. Personally I love treatments and I'll always welcome a gift of a massage!

Boys can be an absolute nightmare to buy presents for, mainly because so many things they like are so expensive! Gadgets, cars, weird electronic things – hardly pocket change, really. They're even trickier to buy fashion presents for because, despite most of them claiming they don't care about fashion, I find they are often pickier than the girls. The things they notice include how baggy the jeans are, what exact shape the trainers are, what the logo on the hoodie is. But I have found that almost all boys like vintage T-shirts and hoodies, and these are not only really easy to

find, but they're generally pretty cheap. Just go to any market, vintage shop, or sometimes even really good record shops and you will almost certainly be able to find them. Definitely no over-logo-ed T-shirts that cost £400. And if your boyfriend or husband likes those, now is the time to wean him off them – unless, of course, they're cool vintage ones, which are very different from designer-designer pieces. If you can spend a little more and are abroad, check out boutiques such as Colette in Paris and 10 Corso Como in Milan for unusual and fun little gadgets, designer accessories and interesting books of photographs too, as most men love these. Urban Outfitters is also good for boy-orientated bits and bobs.

There are now so many good children's clothes around that kids are pretty easy to buy for. Gap do brilliant things for babies and kids and I really like Zara too. H&M do great stuff and Petit Bateau is, of course, a classic. Marks & Spencer is always reliable for kids' underwear and nightwear. Topshop has also started doing a fun fashion range for babies, and another good kids' brand is No Added Sugar. For pretty pieces, Bonpoint, a French company with some branches in the UK, is divine, though a little expensive, and out here in Spain I've bought some beautiful classic clothes for the kids that are incredibly well made – and I truly believe that their leather shoes are the best in the world. With my love for all things denim it will come as no surprise that I'm designing a range of kids' clothes.

Designer kids' clothes are certainly on the indulgent side. As lovely as the outfits are, the kids grow out of them fairly quickly. But they are quite nice to give as baby presents: someone gave Cruz some Baby Dior, which I love, and it was one of my favourite baby gifts. But designer outfits aren't, of course, hugely practical. In less than five minutes my kids will have covered their clothes with mud and grass stains from playing football in the garden. But as a fun little present, they are FABULOUS.

WHERE TO SHOP

Cardigan by Baby Dior

1. FOR GIRLS

candles from Diptyque, The White Company, Jo Malone, Hotel Costes, Manolo Blahnik. Accessories such as Smythson notebooks, Cath Kidston mugs and bags, Prada key fobs, Miu Miu brooches from www.net-a-porter.com, Marc by Marc Jacobs knick-knacks, Missoni scarves, Marc Jacobs purses. Bath products from Nars, MAC, Laura Mercier, Origins, Miller Harris. Home-ware from Zara Home. Treatments from Dermalogica, Elemis, SKII, Crème de la Mer, Cowshed and Bliss

2. FOR BOYS

Paul Smith, Louis Vuitton and Christian Dior for designer accessories, vintage hoodies and T-shirts

3. FOR KIDS AND BABIES *clothes from Baby Dior, Abercrombie & Fitch, Timberland, Zara, Gap, H&M, Topshop, Petit Bateau*

Pregnancy & Post-pregnancy

Baby bottle and baby booties by BABY DIOR;
Body cream by LAURA MERCIER;
Body cream by MAMA MIO

THE DIFFERENCE BETWEEN THE MATERNITY CLOTHES IN THE SHOPS WHEN I WAS PREGNANT WITH BROOKLYN, AND WHEN I WAS PREGNANT WITH CRUZ IS INCREDIBLE.

THINGS REALLY HAVE BECOME SO MUCH BETTER WITHIN THE PAST DECADE, thanks in no small part to labels like Juicy Couture and Seven who have started doing maternity clothes, proving that just because a woman gets pregnant doesn't mean she abandons her sense of style and also that there is a huge market out there for nice maternity wear. Shops like Blossom and 9 London have jumped on this trend and pushed it forward by some way, offering fashionable clothes and even having some designers make up special maternity versions of their beautiful dresses and trousers.

But for the longest time, maternity clothes were pretty much a disaster zone – all those baggy trousers and silly frock tops. After all, just because I'm pregnant doesn't mean I want to look like Demis Roussos. Yes, of course, it's harder being bothered to make an effort when you feel like a two-tonne whale, but that is precisely the reason why brands should make nice, easy-to-wear clothes that help pregnant women to feel good about themselves, not some horrible tent dress that makes them look like a walking mountain.

Some women really love being pregnant, and I know a lot of men find it very sexy.

209

But, personally, though I love having kids I find the pregnancy part tricky. It certainly has not helped matters that in the past so few maternity clothes took into account what actually happens to a woman's body when she's pregnant. For a start, it's not just your tummy and boobs that get bigger but sometimes also your hips, your bottom and often your back. Even your face can change shape and sometimes your skin tone alters so that your make-up starts to look all weird – nobody warned me about that one! So it's not enough making dresses that have room at the front – they have to make room for everything else. And when they don't, well, I can tell you it really doesn't make a pregnant woman feel too good to be walking around in jackets and tops that really squeeze her around her ribs. That's why I fell so in love with ponchos when I was pregnant with Cruz, my third baby: they were one of the few things I could find that had room for my tummy, my boobs and my back.

Some maternity jeans can be problematic too: often they just have elastic in the front but no allowance on the sides for your expanding hips. Also, putting the elastic in the front means that people see that right away, which, purely on a fashion basis, is not particularly attractive. So, instead, whenever I'm pregnant I just make my own maternity jeans by taking a normal pair, cutting V shapes in the side by the pockets and stitching elastic there. That way, I keep the normal zipper fly in front and that is a lot nicer-looking than a big strip of elastic.

The keys to getting through pregnancy and feeling stylish are, first, not to think you suddenly have to buy into the cliché of how a pregnant woman should dress (i.e. frumpy tent dresses and smock tops) and, secondly, to play up the parts of your body you feel fine about and be more discreet about the parts you aren't so happy with. Also, for God's sake, don't make any drastic changes to your physical appearance when you're pregnant: I've seen so many pregnant women suddenly decide to dye

I make my own maternity jeans by taking a normal pair, cutting

their hair or cut it all off. But, because you're all hormonal and not thinking straight, nine times out of ten you'll come out of the pregnancy and think, 'What the bloody hell did I do that for?!'

Back to playing up your good parts. Different people swell up in different places – my

I fell so in love with ponchos when I was pregnant with Cruz, my third baby: they were one of the few things I could find that had room for my tummy, my boobs and my back

V shapes in the sides by the pockets and stitching elastic there

Poncho style in pregnancy

211

The number one item I think every pregnant woman needs is a wrap dress. We've already spoken about how useful wrap dresses are generally, but they are totally brilliant when you're pregnant sister had pregnant ears! – but for me, it's the sides of my torso – as I seem to expand mainly outwards – and my lower legs. So I would wear tops, such as sharp jackets or side-skimming tops, that are tailored on the sides to give me a bit of shape but were loose in front, and fitted-leg trousers that I would let out at the top. Similarly, my boobs get so big during my pregnancies that they practically start around my back, and many women's often become really veiny as well and basically look like a map of the motorway network, so wearing a low-cut top would just look totally inappropriate, and not very nice either. This is not about hiding the fact that you're pregnant – I'd have had a hell of a job trying to do that! – but rather finding ways to look and, more importantly, feel confident about your appearance during your pregnancy. After all, you're just having a baby; you don't need to go into hibernation beneath layers of ugly clothes for nine months! And you don't have to totally ditch your usual style; you just have to make a bit of an effort to find clothes that look right but also are roomy enough for your body.

The number one item I think every pregnant woman needs is a wrap dress. We've already spoken about how useful wrap dresses are generally, but they are totally brilliant when you're pregnant. They're adjustable in precisely the places that change during your pregnancy – your back, your boobs, your tummy – and are particularly handy when it comes to breast-feeding. In fact, some women can wear their usual, non-maternity wrap dress for a fair way into their pregnancy, which really helps them to feel both more normal during this time, and also that they haven't become a different person. Wrap dresses are also incredibly flattering to all pregnant women because the cotton jersey just skims over your body as opposed to clinging and making you feel self-conscious. They can be slim-fitting on the sides and expand very subtly in the front. As your boobs get so mammoth towards the end of your pregnancy, nipples the size of hubcaps and everything, a lot of dresses and tops give you an enormous cleavage, which can be really embarrassing, not to mention distracting for others. For that reason, it is essential that you get a good maternity bra. They might look like you could hoist them up and sail yourself across the Atlantic, but never will you be more in need of support than now, with your boobs swelling up and often feeling very tender. As your boobs are changing so much, it is definitely worth getting them re-measured, which you can do in any decent lingerie section of a department store or Mothercare.

Most department stores now sell good maternity bras, especially Marks & Spencer, which has a fantastic selection. Splenda and Bloomin' Marvellous also make very good ones. Always check that your bra has wide straps and a broad side and back for the support.

Back to wrap dresses, they play down your boobs because the material crosses over them, thereby separating them, so there's no cleavage for people to stare down. You can also decide whether you feel more comfortable having the belt over your tummy or under it – it's different for all women as each individual's bump grows differently.

This is one time in your life when little empire-line vests and tops work with a big bust because they act a bit like a protective curtain covering your tummy, but just make sure they are cut big enough for your boobs at the top and long enough to cover your bump. Wear one with your home-made maternity jeans and a fitted leather jacket that you can just leave open at the front and you have a perfect maternity look. Really, you just need your maternity clothes to be practical and that is a very practical outfit in which you don't feel exposed, you have total freedom of movement, nothing's hugging you uncomfortably, and you can run around and just get on with your day in it.

Happily, there are now some maternity fashion ranges that are getting a lot better. Topshop in particular has recently launched an amazing maternity-wear range that is basically the usual Topshop fun fashion but adjusted to suit pregnant women, and other high street stores also have a good selection.

Then there are Blossom and 9 London that I mentioned earlier but they are more expensive. Blossom is particularly good for clothes that aren't maternity per se, but are cut in such a way to accommodate a pregnant figure.

There are some things, though, on which I will not compromise, even if they are impractical. You remember how I said I am a high-heels girl? And remember that I also said you shouldn't change your usual style when you're pregnant? So, yes, I do still wear my stilettos when I'm pregnant, but I'm certainly not recommending it for anyone else, and most women will opt for simple flats. This is particularly true if they suffer from any kind of back pain, which is a miserably common problem for pregnant women. I remember when I was heavily pregnant with Romeo, my mum and I took Brooklyn to Legoland, of all places, in the middle of August, and there I was, tottering around in my high heels. Now that was, I admit, incredibly

One thing you can do during pregnancy to make yourself feel better is to indulge yourself with some beauty treatments

*Japanese Camellia Oil
by Elemis*

ELEMIS'S JAPANESE CAMELLIA OIL IS REALLY GREAT FOR PREVENTING STRETCH MARKS

uncomfortable, but, like I said, I just refuse to accept that I have to totally change when I'm pregnant.

Another thing that definitely does not change, pregnant or not, is my opinion of cropped tops and I think they look even worse than usual when pregnant women wear them. Personally, I would feel so exposed and just not right having my bump so much on show. And it looks to me like the baby inside seems so unprotected. This may sound strange to some people but it just makes me feel really uncomfortable.

One thing you can do during pregnancy to make yourself feel better is to indulge yourself with some beauty treatments. Just slathering yourself in really delicious body moisturizers will make you feel happier in your skin – and sexier – and can be a good way to help prevent stretch marks.

Massages are amazingly good for you too, as is the occasional facial, but just make sure you check with your GP first and always tell the beauty therapist that you're pregnant because some products can get in the bloodstream and may not be good for the baby. During all my pregnancies, the one product I really relied on was Elemis's Japanese Camellia Oil which is really great for preventing stretch marks and is one of the few aromatherapy oils you can put on yourself when pregnant. I would just cover myself in it, really massaging it into my tummy, my bottom, my thighs and my boobs and, honestly, that stuff really works. Space NK does some nice maternity products as well but ALWAYS check with your doctor first before trying out products during your pregnancy.

After giving birth, I do tend just to wear tracksuits and pyjamas for six weeks. But even when you emerge from that cocoon of the immediate aftermath of the birth, there is no question that post-pregnancy dressing can be as tricky as dressing during pregnancy. I remember a time, about three months after I had Romeo and we were still living in Manchester, David and I went to an Usher concert for our first night out since the birth. I got all dressed up in my nice clothes and was really looking forward to being a bit glamorous for an hour or two. But just as the concert began and the crowds were all screaming, my boobs started leaking like nobody's business. So I spent most of my big night out mopping up my soggy front.

You can get little nipple cover-ups from Mothercare and Boots so you don't find yourself cleaning milk off your dress all evening. They aren't very alluring but they're better than the bowl-shaped things I've seen in some chemists': you're supposed to somehow stick these to your boobs and they catch the milk, then you empty them out at the end of the day. Can you imagine? First of all, you'd look like you have the world's biggest nipples, and secondly they're so large you could probably pick up Sky TV with them. Possibly the best thing you can do for yourself after having a baby is to go back and have, yes, more beauty treatments, but, again, check with your GP first about when you can start having them as everyone's needs are different. Just getting a foot massage from a friend or your partner will make such a huge difference, not only for the physical relief but also just to get a few minutes of self-indulgence. Foot massages are also really fantastic for getting rid of the water retention that many women get around their ankles after giving birth.

I used to love getting ready in the mornings: having my bath, doing my hair, choosing what to wear – I had my whole little routine. But when you become a mum you just don't have as much time. There were some jokes a while ago in which people claimed I'd said I'd never read a book. What actually happened was I gave an interview to a Spanish publication and I said that once you have three kids you hardly have time to finish a book, which, as any mum will tell you, is perfectly true. 'Lost in translation' springs to mind.

Because kids do kind of take over your life, it is essential for you and your partner to make sure you take a little time out for just the two of you, whether this means just going out for supper together or spending the night in a hotel or simply curling up for a proper chat. It can be all too easy for the kids to become the focal point of your relationship and so it's really important not to forget one another. As any parent will know, your priorities will change when you have a family.

And as well as your life changing, a lot of people say that their style changed when they became a mum. For me, at least, I don't think that's true but I do think it's changed as I've got older. I think my look now is less contrived and that reflects how – as most people do – I have become more relaxed in myself and make fewer mistakes as I've got older.

WHAT TO BUY

1. MATERNITY WEAR
ponchos, wrap dresses, tailored jackets, empire-line vests and tops, maternity bras

2. BEAUTY TREATMENTS
Bliss Vanilla and Bergamot Body Butter, Elemis Japanese Camellia Oil, vitamin E oil

Lingerie

Bra and knickers by MARKS & SPENCER;
Cotton boyshorts by CALVIN KLEIN UNDERWEAR

YOU DON'T HAVE TO MATCH YOUR BRA TO YOUR KNICKERS!

A WHILE AGO IN A FASHION MAGAZINE, I SAID THAT I DON'T THINK YOU HAVE TO MATCH YOUR BRA TO YOUR KNICKERS. You'd have thought I said the world was flat for all the fuss it caused. Of course they don't have to match! I have other things to think about than whether my bra is properly coordinated with my knickers.

Of course I adore beautiful lingerie. But there's no need to get carried away about things that really don't matter, particularly when they're just not practical. I'm all up for sexy lingerie in the bedroom, but for under clothes you need to be more realistic and get something that will give you a nice shape and proper support. It's ridiculous to wear a frilly bra beneath a T-shirt, for example, as the lace will bump up through the material and make you look like you have four boobs. Instead, get a practical bra that will give you a nice bustline. My favourites are Calvin Klein Underwear's T-shirt bras, which I call my teabag bras because they just look like two simple little teabags on a strap. Then, if you want to feel a bit sexier, you can wear your seductive frilly knickers with it. They may not match, but it does allow you to be both practical and sexy.

But never mind the whole matching debate, the first thing to pay attention to with bras is the size, and I strongly recommend that you get measured properly by a professional. So many women in this country wear the wrong size of bra, and you can tell. Wearing the wrong size does absolutely nothing for your bust: often it minimizes it, or if the cups are too big they'll poke out slightly under your clothes so that you look like you have two little domes under there. People often get their back measurement wrong too, so that the strap either digs in badly or drapes awkwardly and doesn't give you any support. Most lingerie shops now have a measuring service, as do many lingerie sections in department stores. Probably the best-known place to be measured is Rigby & Peller. They are next to Harrods and are the approved suppliers to the Queen. Well, if it's good enough for her, it's good enough for the rest of us.

Once you know how many practical and sexy bras and knickers you need, and you know your size, there are so many good places to buy your lingerie. For practical bras and knickers, I've already mentioned Calvin Klein Underwear, who I really do think make the most comfortable and best plain underwear all round. Bonds from Australia make nice cotton boy-pants, which are practical and cute. Good old Marks & Spencer, of course, do great knickers: their lace and cotton boy-pants are fab. And to give them credit, their strapless bras really do work and last for absolutely ages, and you can bung them in the washing machine without any worries that they'll come out all mangled. Playtex make great simple and practical bras, as they have done for decades, and are just the thing to wear under T-shirts, V-necks and pullovers. They are, though, it has to be said, passion killers! Petit Bateau's are so sweet and French and comfortable, and Elle Macpherson Intimates are also favourites of mine, with beautiful and practical pieces. Don't forget to always wear a good sports bra when you're exercising as you don't want to trip over your boobs on the running machine or end up with two black eyes!

There are a lot of good websites now too, such as www.figleaves.com and www.chantilly.co.uk, which is a real boon for anyone who finds lingerie shopping embarrassing, or just doesn't have the time. Just make sure you know your size.

For sexy lingerie, there is even more choice, mainly thanks to Agent Provocateur, which was the first shop in this country to show that sexy knickers didn't have to mean nasty tacky stuff but could be really beautiful. It is my favourite lingerie place along with La Perla, but both are expensive. Fifi Chachnil make just the cutest, flirtiest pieces that give you a great shape. You can buy them in concessions in England but if you're in Paris you should check out the gorgeous little shop.

I strongly recommend that you get measured properly by a professional. So many women in this country wear the wrong size of bra

Bra by Coco Ribbon

Seductive

Myla

Myla does a great mix of both super-sexy satin pieces and more practical cotton briefs.

Agent Provocateur

Agent Provocateur was the first place in this country to show that sexy knickers didn't have to mean nasty tacky stuff but could be really beautiful

Sexy

Girlie

Agent Provocateur

Even if string really isn't your thing, Agent Provocateur has some great girly and more modest pieces. Their frilly 50s-style knickers are great.

Practical & Pretty

Marks & Spencer

Good old Marks & Spencer do great knickers: their lace and cotton boy-pants are fab, and they also do good flirty knickers in their Autograph collection

In the States I love popping into Victoria's Secret and, no, not just for the name. It's got some beautiful bras, knickers, nightwear, as well as practical pieces and lots of other accessories. There are now a lot of Agent Provocateur-like ranges in Britain that sell gorgeous bits and bobs, such as Myla, Soshe and Jane Delacy, which are very beautiful.

Lingerie really does make a great fashion present that most men love to give. I'm so lucky that David likes getting it for me and, even more fortunately, I think he has very good taste. But then, we have been together for a long time and he knows me very well. If you're in a younger relationship, or your boyfriend is just not very clued-up about this kind of thing, it might be worth giving him a bit of gentle guidance, either by letting him accompany you on a lingerie-shopping trip or simply by subtly and tactfully offering a few guiding words.

In bed, the best options are simple silky nighties or pyjamas. For silky nighties, Victoria's Secret make gorgeous ones, as do Agent Provocateur and La Perla, and Elle Macpherson's pyjamas are fantastic, particularly the vest tops with boy-shorts, which come in great fabrics. Pretty much her entire range is just perfect for wandering around the house in on Sunday mornings, and a much better option than a tracksuit. Calvin Klein Underwear and Ralph Lauren both do cute vests and boy-shorts, which would be ideal for that too. Topshop and Agent Provocateur make gorgeous little silken camisoles with matching shorts. Marks & Spencer's also offers excellent machine-washable nightwear. GapBody often does sweet pyjamas, with long trousers and little vest tops that are really cosy in the winter and very good if you feel a bit too exposed in boy-shorts. Or you can go the other way and wear a pair of

In bed, the best options are simple silk nighties or pyjamas. For silky

pretty boxers with a matching long-sleeved top.

For dressing gowns, I just really want a big fluffy one that I can snuggle into, though not a full-length one because I trip over them. Just a cosy knee-length terry-cloth dressing gown will do perfectly and you can always find them in any department store like John Lewis or Habitat. The White Company is really great for nice bedding, bathrobes and scented candles, and not too expensive, either.

nighties, Agent Provocateur and La Perla make gorgeous ones . . .

IN THE SUMMER, BECAUSE IT GETS SO HOT IN SPAIN, I SWITCH OVER TO LITTLE SILKY DRESSING GOWNS, WHICH YOU CAN GET IN AGENT PROVOCATEUR, OR KIMONOS, WHICH YOU CAN FIND IN VINTAGE OR JAPANESE SHOPS

In the summer, because it gets so hot in Spain, I switch over to little silky dressing gowns, which you can get in Agent Provocateur, or even kimonos, which you often find in vintage stores or Japanese shops. But silky ones in general are pretty widely available in the bed or bath section in any department store.

For slippers, a lot of people will probably find my tastes quite surprising. Yeah, those high-heeled marabou pumps look rather fabulous but they're hardly going to work when you're running about and getting the Frosties ready for the kids. Instead, I just love little flat ones with patterns on them, like stars or little monkeys. My mum gets them for me at Marks & Spencer and sends them to Madrid so I don't have to be deprived even though I now live in a country that, shockingly, doesn't have a Marks. Really, all I ever want as a present is a pair of pyjamas and some slippers. Well, and maybe some nice lingerie from David too, if he insists.

Those high-heeled marabou pumps look rather fabulous but they're hardly going to work when you're running about and getting the Frosties ready for the kids

WHERE TO SHOP

1. PRACTICAL UNDIES

Calvin Klein Underwear, Bonds, Marks & Spencer, Gap, Elle Macpherson Intimates, Bodas, American Apparel, www.figleaves.com

2. SEXY UNDIES
Agent Provocateur, Victoria's Secret, Fifi Chachnil, Marks & Spencer Autograph collection, La Perla, Topshop, Damaris, Myla, Elle Macpherson Intimates, Mimi Holiday, Coco Ribbon, www.figleaves.com

3. NIGHTWEAR
Victoria's Secret, Agent Provocateur, Calvin Klein Underwear, Ralph Lauren, Gap Body, Marks & Spencer, www.figleaves.com

4. SILK BATHROBES

Agent Provocateur, Japanese stores, www.figleaves.com

Shopping

SHOPPING SHOULD BE ONE OF THE MOST PLEASURABLE ACTIVITIES IN THE WHOLE WORLD.

SO IT'S SUCH A SHAME IT CAN SOMETIMES BE DIFFICULT.

One of the hardest things is knowing how much money to spend on something. Nobody wants to feel ripped off, but, equally, buying something very cheap and badly made can be just as much of a waste of money. I've talked about this a little throughout the book but the general rule of thumb is that for anything that depends on cut (such as trousers and tailored jackets), quality (like smart accessories, for example leather bags) or is an investment buy (like LBDs and coats) it is worth paying a little more; for simple basics, head for the high street.

HIGH END

1. BRAS *Agent Provocateur, Fifi Chachnil, Damaris, La Perla*

2. TAILORED JACKETS *Alexander McQueen, Balenciaga, Chloe, Dolce & Gabbana, Gucci*

3. COATS *Azzedine Alaïa, Burberry, Dolce & Gabbana, Donna Karan, Lanvin, Prada, Roberto Cavalli*

4. TAILORED TROUSERS *Balenciaga, Chloe, Dolce & Gabbana, Gucci, Viktor & Rolf*

5. HANDBAGS AND SHOES *Anya Hindmarch, Burberry, Chanel, Chloe, Fendi, Hermès, Manolo Blahnik, Marc Jacobs, Mulberry, Prada, VBH, Yves Saint Laurent*

6. GOOD JEANS *Citizens of Humanity, Habitual, Notify, Rock & Republic, Superfine*

7. BOOTS *Chanel, Chloe, Christian Louboutin, Gucci, Jimmy Choo, Manolo Blahnik*

8. SPECIAL SHOES *Chanel, Christian Louboutin, Georgina Goodman, Jimmy Choo, Manolo Blahnik, Pierre Hardy*

HIGH STREET

1. T-SHIRTS, V-NECK & POLO-NECK JUMPERS
I love Topshop for all of these, American Apparel

2. FITTED TOPS *check the length so they don't gape above your waistband (anywhere)*

3. BLOUSES *Topshop, Mango, H&M, Miss Selfridge, Zara, Whistles*

4. FLIP-FLOPS *Accessorize, Topshop, Gap*

5. TIGHTS *Topshop, Marks & Spencer, John Lewis*

6. KNICKERS *Marks & Spencer, Topshop, Miss Selfridge*

7. PARKAS *Topshop, Mango, Zara, Laurence Corner, Jungle & Rokit, Miss Selfridge*

8. SUMMER DRESSES *Karen Millen, Oasis, Warehouse, Topshop, Reiss, Zara, Miss Selfridge, H&M, Whistles, Florence & Fred, Primark, Peacocks, Matalan*

9. SHORTS, T-SHIRTS & VESTS *Abercrombie & Fitch, Gap, Petit Bateau, American Apparel, Topshop*

10. BELTS *Topshop*

11. CARDIGANS *Whistles, Zara, H&M, Marks & Spencer*

12. PARTY SHOES *Faith, Shellys, Karen Millen, Russell & Bromley*

13. DAY SHOES *Topshop, Faith, Zara, Kurt Geiger*

The majority of your wardrobe can easily come from the high street. It is just incredible how much nearly all of the shops have improved, from Topshop to Primark to Matalan. I must admit, I really do miss the British high street. At least, here in Madrid, we have a Topshop, which I go to all the time, and, of course, Mango and Zara, which everyone loves. Sometimes I think the main reason my friends from England come to visit me out here is to go to Zara! Seriously, as soon as they get off the plane they're practically running to the biggest outlet they can find. Without question, it does a brilliant take on designer clothes, which is great as it means everyone can try the Chloe or Dolce look this season, or whatever designer they fancy. My friends all call it Dolce & Gazzara. That's all I ever hear when they come to visit: 'Let's go to Dolce & Gazzara!'

For cool one-off pieces, vintage is obviously the way to go. If you're in the market for something really special when you're shopping for vintage, look for labels that have a real history, such as Lanvin, Versace and Valentino. Vintage clothes are getting much more popular these days, mainly, I think, because the high street is dominated by a few massive chains and that can lead to many people looking the same, so a lot of women are looking for something more individual. Plus, a lot of celebrities are wearing vintage dresses to red-carpet events, not least because they can then be sure that no one else will be wearing their dress, and the magazines have really picked up on that.

But you may find vintage shopping quite intimidating, and understandably so: all the clothes seem to be in a jumble; it can be hard to tell if the dress will make you look like Julia Roberts or Pat Butcher; the prices can seem hideous; and the sales assistant might look at you like you're somehow defective if you can't tell that something is an original Azzaro. People who work in vintage shops are generally very knowledgeable about the clothes and fashion history (this, as I mentioned earlier, is what differentiates vintage stores, which choose their stock carefully, from second-hand shops). One thing that can be frustrating is that some vintage shops don't put prices on the clothes, which makes me suspect they just make them up on the spot. I did have a rare but miserable experience in a vintage shop recently when I asked how much something was. The shop owner looked at me and you could see him thinking, 'Hmmm, Victoria Beckham, hmmm . . .' And then

Vintage shopping with friends at What Goes Around Comes Around in New York

Patricia Field the superstar Costume Designer working on Sex and the City has always been such an inspiration to me

he said, with a totally straight face, 'Five thousand pounds.' Five thousand pounds!

The trick is to go to trusted vintage places, and often the best guidance on that front is simply through word of mouth. Some great vintage shops are Virginia, Orsini, One of a Kind, One, Rellik, and Steinberg and Tolkein in London; Didier Ludot in Paris; What Goes Around Comes Around, Screaming Mimi's and Resurrection in New York and Decades in LA. Importantly, the people who work in all these shops are really nice and helpful, which is the sure sign of a good shop as it shows they have faith in their merchandise. At What Goes Around Comes Around in New York, for example, they kindly took me to see their archive, which was so totally inspiring. I found lots of original Azzedine Alaïa pieces, and I really do think that Azzedine Alaïa is probably the best when it comes to cutting clothes properly so that they suit a woman's shape. Just seeing all these amazing original pieces really helped me to understand what I should be looking for when buying clothes, and how to put great outfits together, which is what you should always get from a vintage store. Patricia Field in New York is another one of my real favourites and she has just opened her second shop. I first met Patricia before she became the superstar Costume Designer working on *Sex and the City*, and she has always been such an inspiration to me. Her shop in New York is just brilliant: you can find anything there, from tiny hotpants to tutus to leotards with attached cardigans. I know, it all sounds totally nuts, but remember this is the woman who showed us how great crazy could look on Carrie. Plus, it's just such fun to rummage about in there.

Vintage shops often introduce you to styles that you never see anywhere else, just because they don't make outfits like that any more, and it is great to wear something totally original. When some friends and I went to What Goes Around Comes Around in New York recently we found some fantastic original 70s Ossie Clark dresses. It was so interesting to see these original pieces, particularly as back in England Topshop had just launched its range by Celia Birtwell, who was Clark's wife and designed most of his prints. There is something pretty exciting about seeing the original pieces that inspired a line that can still sell out in literally less than ten minutes. Similarly, finding vintage Valentino is always exciting as his pieces somehow never look dated – they are timelessly elegant. Just think of how gorgeous Julia Roberts looked in her vintage Valentino dress when she won her Oscar.

With regard to second-hand and charity shops, you can also find some real treasures, particularly in posh areas, such as Kensington in London (you wouldn't believe what some of the locals give away!), and at Portobello Road market on Fridays, especially under the arches (don't bother with Saturdays – too crowded with tourists). Car-boot and jumble sales can also come up with amazing goods and the prices are low, of course, because there's no store taking any cut.

But there is no denying that both vintage and second-hand shopping take longer than normal shopping as you really have to go through the rails to squirrel out the good stuff. So don't ever go if you're in a rush as it will just put you in a bad mood and you'll be put off vintage shopping for good.

Of course, going to a department store is probably the easiest way to shop, especially if you've got the kids in tow. You just park the car and get everything sorted, from having your nails done to picking up some clothes and replenishing your make-up supplies. Selfridges in the UK are particularly strong on stocking innovative, lesser-known brands as well as the big classics, and have terrific themed parties. Harrods has an excellent range of stock and their personal shopping is very, very good. I also love shopping at Harvey Nichols and think it's great for more edgy pieces. Liberty's is just a beautiful store, making it a real pleasure to stop by. Barney's in the States is one of my real favourites and is great for both super-glamorous labels as well as younger, more urban ones, and I also always check out Bergdorf Goodman when I'm in Manhattan. Sticking with the States, Fred Segal in LA is one of the best boutique stores in the world, and certainly one of the most fabulously glam, as you'd expect from its Melrose Avenue location. Everyone from Gwyneth Paltrow to Madonna has been photographed toting a Fred Segal shopping bag. Bloomingdales, Saks and Macy's are also worth a visit. In Spain, so many people rely on El Corte Ingles, which has really lovely food, good basic clothes and a nice beauty hall.

*Azzedine Alaïa
and me in Paris*

David recently took me on a surprise trip to Paris, which was so exciting. The icing on the cake was when he took me to the Azzedine Alaïa showroom because he knows just how much I love that label

If you are in the market for something a bit more expensive, you could try little boutiques as they often stock young designers you've never heard of, or just really unusual pieces. Even if you're not going to buy anything they are almost always so inspiring. In London, Browns on South Molton Street is probably the most well known and sells unusual designer pieces. It was the store that first spotted John Galliano. It is very expensive, but it has a cheaper concession, Browns Focus, which is, handily and happily, just across the road. Matches SPY, in Notting Hill, works in a similar way, selling slightly younger and cheaper labels than Matches, which is just opposite, as well as having branches around London. Other great boutiques in London include Souvenir in Soho, Diverse, Sefton and Start in the east end. I also love Colette and Maria Luisa in Paris; Scoop and Jeffrey's in New York, and 10 Corso Como in Milan. Many of them have things like unusual music, home ware, books and even cosmetics, so they're really like mini department stores, and, like I said, you can get so much from them just by walking around and looking.

I am very fortunate that in my position I have been able to go to designers' personal studios, and they have taught me so much about how to put clothes together

à victoria et DAVid Beckam
mon admiration et affection
Azzedine Alaïa

and how clothes that really fit should feel on your body. For example, David recently took me on a surprise trip to Paris, which was so exciting. The icing on the cake was when he took me to the Azzedine Alaïa showroom because he knows just how much I love that label and, amazingly, Mr Alaïa himself was there! I was so nervous but he turned out to be such a kind man, as well as being a genius and absolute master. Anyway, he really took me through how he cuts his clothes so exactly and how they should fit and make you feel. And if you're going to learn these things from anyone, I have to say that Mr Alaïa is a pretty good place to start: it's hard to think of a better teacher than someone who himself was once taught by Christian Dior.

As a mum, though, I don't have as much time as I used to, to stroll around the shops. The internet is great for food and book shopping. My favourite website for clothes and accessories is www.net-a-porter.com. I love it for special buys as the items arrive so quickly, are so beautifully wrapped and the company has a fantastic returns policy, but they mainly stock expensive labels. Many high street stores have also jumped on the internet bandwagon.

The mail-order catalogue La Redoute, which I mentioned earlier, is also extremely convenient and covers the French high street. It has good, well-made basic styles with classic French simplicity, as well as seasonal collaborations with designers.

But you know, the truth is that I prefer to feel the clothes and see how things are made because it is so important to check out the quality before buying. I've had friends who've had to spend more money on alterations than they spent on the item itself, and that's just crazy. Plus, everyone knows that sizes vary between labels. So, for these reasons, be wary of mail-order and internet buying.

But the worst shopping experience has got to be the high street on a Saturday afternoon. That really is the seventh circle of hell. It's just so crowded, the clothes are all over the shop because so many people pick things up and leave them wherever, the queue at the till is enormous, you can't get into the changing room so you end up buying things you haven't tried on and they then don't fit properly and not all

MY FAVOURITE WEBSITE FOR CLOTHES AND ACCESSORIES IS WWW.NET-A-PORTER.COM

Belt by Mulberry

I try to be disciplined and only ever buy things that I know I'll truly

shops take returns and, well . . . Most high-street shops these days are open on Sundays as well, and it is much more peaceful then so I recommend waiting just that extra day.

But going back to the changing-room issue, always make sure you've looked around the store thoroughly before going to the changing room so you get everything that you like in one go – no one can be bothered to go to the changing room more than once, taking off their boots and jeans. And that's another point: if you know you're going shopping that day, in the morning make sure you put on clothes that are easy to take on and off, like just a dress and sandals, or trousers and a jumper. Things like jeans, boots and layers are a total pain to have to take off and put back on eight times in a row.

Shopping on your own is very enjoyable but I think it's good to go with someone who you know will be honest. As ever, David, my mum and my sister are the best for that and, because they know me so well, they're also good at spotting things that would suit me that I might have missed. In fact, I trust them so much that Louise often phones me from London and says that she's found something that she knows I'd like so should she buy it for me and I can pay her back. I always say yes. I don't think I've ever disagreed with any of their shopping recommendations.

Taking a man shopping can be a bit of a challenge as they almost always want to leave as soon as possible – and who can blame them? There they are, stuck in a shop full of screaming girls chucking vest tops and multipacks of knickers about the place – it might sound quite sexy when put like that but I think any man would agree that it's not. Having said that, I have to add that I'm lucky that David is quite interested in fashion and he knows how much I love clothes, so he will put in the time to shop with me.

I try to be disciplined and only ever buy things that I know I'll truly wear. Despite what some people may think, I don't go into shops and say, 'I'll have that in every colour.' When I do decide I like something, I'll pretty much always ask the shop to put it on hold for me so I can go away and think about it. You'd be surprised how often the insane desire for something fades as soon as you leave the shop and step back into the sunlight. It is a really good way to stop yourself from making a silly impulse purchase, and if you actually make the effort to go back to that shop the next day, you'll know you must really want the item.

wear. I don't go into shops and say, I'll have that in every colour

Make-up & Hair

*Perfume by CREED, MARC JACOBS AND MILLER HARRIS;
Lipstick and gloss by ESTEE LAUDER; Brush by TRISH
MCEVOY; eyelash curlers by SHU UEMURA*

MY EARLIEST MAKE-UP MEMORY IS MY MUM RUBBING A BIT OF LIPSTICK ON MY CHEEKS BEFORE I WENT TO SCHOOL, TO TRY TO MAKE ME LOOK PERKIER IN THE MORNINGS.

BUT I STARTED TO GET INTO IT MYSELF FROM AN EARLY AGE. I CERTAINLY HAD MY EXPERIMENTAL YEARS AND – NOW BEAR IN MIND THESE WERE THE 80S – my first ever lipstick was called Twilight Teaser by Boots No. 17 and it was an iridescent purple. Classy, don't you think? I never could resist a bit of iridescence. As a kid, instead of playing with dolls, I would make collections of sequins and diamantés – anything girly and shiny. In fact, I probably haven't changed that much.

But, truth be told, when I was younger I used to struggle with make-up because of my skin. For one thing, because I've got an olive skin tone, I often go a bit pasty in the winter and that never looks good, so I have to make special efforts then – hence my mum with her lipstick at the ready.

But the biggest hurdle was, of course, when I had bad skin as a teenager. This was really what propelled me towards the make-up counter from a pretty early age. When I was about thirteen, every day before school I would cover my face in

Make-up & Hair

259

Putting too much make-up on - whoever or whatever you are - really is the worst mistake you can make. So make sure you never apply it in bad light; find somewhere that mimics natural sunlight

concealer, and every day the teachers would make me scrub it off in the toilet.

Teenage acne is definitely not a stroll in the park. Seriously, when I was a teenager I had so many spots I could barely put a pin between them. It was just awful. Finally, I went to a doctor to see what was wrong and it turned out I had some bad food allergies, and as soon as I changed my diet my skin totally cleared up.

I have been extremely fortunate in that I've never had any scars from the acne, but that really is the luck of the draw.

I am still very careful with my skin. I would never claim to be a skin and make-up specialist, so all I'm doing is telling you what I've found works best for me. For a start, I am religious about keeping my skin clean, giving it lots of scrubs and making sure I always take off all my make-up at the end of the night – Johnson's baby wipes are great for that. I avoid overly oily moisturizers and use deep-cleaning cleansers. Vitamin E oil is also very good for soothing skin, and Jo Malone does a great Vitamin E cream. When you have spots, it is tempting to slather them with concealer but, actually, this often makes them much worse because all that concealer will clog the pores. Really, if you have a big spot, sometimes the best thing to do is to accept it and leave it as it is because it will clear up much quicker. But if you really need concealer, MAC do a wide variety of tones that aren't too heavy on the skin.

When I studied dance as a teenager, it was drummed into me right from the start that you have to have nice fingernails and nice hair, and I think it's just ingrained in me now. I'm always really strict with myself about grooming. But that doesn't mean I haven't occasionally gone very wrong. When I look back at photographs of the Spice Girls I see a lot of make-up mistakes, but I think many pop stars suffer from the same problem: because you're working so hard and are getting so tired you just plaster on the make-up to cover the signs of stress and tiredness. So your make-up gets thicker and thicker and your hair gets bigger and bigger and you just end up looking like the creature from the Black Lagoon. Putting too much make-up on – whoever or whatever you are – really is the worst mistake you can make. So make sure you never apply it in bad light; find somewhere that mimics natural sunlight.

When I'm home I just tend to do my nails and whatever else I fancy after the kids have gone to bed and David's away playing football, as the rest of the time I want to be with my family. And there are some beauty treatments that you should definitely only do when you're on your own. For example, I'm a great believer in well-kept feet and hands. So one night I decided to try out this lovely foot and hand treatment from Bliss. I scrubbed my feet properly, put the cream on them and on my hands, and then put on these little gloves they provide to let the cream soak in properly. So there I was, in my dressing gown, watching TV with what looked like oven mitts on my hands and my feet, all creamed up and drinking a cup of tea, and I must have looked completely ridiculous. So I'd recommend saving that one for when your man is away!

Fake tanning is another thing to do when you're on your own. When David's away, I'll apply the St Tropez. Put it on at night before getting into bed.

I love face packs too, and try to do two a week, usually using La Prairie's Cellular Balancing Mask or Dermalogica's Multivitamin Power Recovery Masque, which I call my little ambulance in a tube. But that's another one I try to leave for when I'm alone as face packs really can make you look like an axe murderer in some low-rent horror movie.

The Body Shop is one of my favourite places for skin and body products. It's always such a pleasure going into the stores as they all smell so nice and familiar. Their exfoliating gloves – which are basically Brillo pads for your hands that you take with you into the shower to give your skin a really good scrub, getting rid of all the dead skin cells and boosting your circulation – are the best I've ever found. Their wood-handled body brushes are great too: just brushing your skin in an upward motion towards your heart before your shower will get your circulation going, and that helps to minimize cellulite.

Self-tanning spray
by St Tropez

Another one of my true staple products is Elizabeth Arden's Eight Hour Cream. There's no frilliness about it, it just does what it says and does it really well – as you'd expect of a product that was originally invented to be used on the shanks of race horses to soothe their irritated skin, which gives a sense of just how moisturizing it is. It's extremely thick so you need only a tiny amount, meaning it lasts for ages, and is the best thing in the world for chapped lips, elbows and knees, and even faces on long-haul, dehydrating flights. You can also put a small slick on your eyelashes to bring them out a little bit more.

In terms of other basics, every girl needs a pair of tweezers and the best by far are by Tweezerman. Prada's Shielding Lip Balm is another thing I almost always have on me.

On the days when I have the time (and believe me I can do this very quickly), my morning routine is shower, facial cleanser, toner, moisturizer, neck cream, eye cream, foot cream, hand cream, make-up (if going out), and then the same in the evening, minus the make-up, of course. For the shower, I love shower gels and bubble baths from Boots, especially Radox and

Aero Bronze

INSTANT SELF-TANNING AIR SPRAY

Step 3

ST.TROPEZ

LA BRUME AUTO-BRONZANTE INSTANTÉE

170 mL ℮ 6 FI OZ

Eight Hour Cream by Elizabeth Arden

ANOTHER ONE OF MY TRUE STAPLE PRODUCTS IS ELIZABETH ARDEN'S EIGHT HOUR CREAM. THERE'S NO FRILLINESS ABOUT IT, IT JUST DOES WHAT IT SAYS AND DOES IT REALLY WELL

Dove. My hairdresser gave me a product called Caviar Anti Aging conditioner by Alterna, which really keeps your hair moisturized and smooth, even in Madrid in August. Washing your hair too regularly can strip it of oils and make it go all flyaway or, worse, frizzy, which is why some professional hairstylists recommend using shampoo only every other day or two.

One of the things Geri taught me when we were in the Spice Girls was that just before you get out of the shower you should turn the temperature down and get a blast of freezing-cold water. It makes your skin look really taut and smooth too and is great for the circulation, but it is not very pleasant, I have to say, and it is something you have to force yourself to do.

As for body scrubs, Origins' Paradise Found is great, and Bliss and Laura Mercier do some really gorgeously scented ones, as does Marc Jacobs, whose scrub also gives your skin a tiny hint of glitter. The nice thing about body scrubs is that they are a delicious way to help wake yourself up and get the circulation going, and a

Make-up & Hair

But, really, like most women, I prefer baths to showers, lying in a big sudsy tub, reading some magazines, listening to the radio and getting some time to myself

much more fun way to do it than dry body brushing. Plus, of course, they are great for exfoliating, which always makes everyone's skin look better. I know, it's really tempting not to exfoliate when you have a tan as you want to keep your colour for as long as possible, but, really, it's a choice between your tan going all patchy and flaking off or just tackling it yourself properly. So make sure you give yourself a good scrub at least twice a week when you're on holiday – after all, that is when you want your skin looking its best.

Scented body washes are a lovely way to help wake yourself up in the shower in the morning. A nice blast of pretty perfume, combined with giving yourself a good clean, is a much more pleasant way to come to consciousness than having the radio alarm blast your ear off. Miller Harris does really nice body washes, particularly the Citron Citron one, which smells so fresh and lemony. Chantecaille does a range of delicate floral ones and Slatkin makes some with really unusual fragrances. For unscented washes, Origins' A Perfect World creamy body cleanser makes your skin squeak, it gets it so clean. Kiehl's has made a shower range of its brilliant Crème de Corps, and their Crème de Corps Nurturing Body Washing Cream is a great way to clean your skin and moisturize it at the same time.

THE BODY SHOP®

COCOA BUTTER
VERY DRY SKIN

BEURRE DE CACAO
PEAUX TRÈS SÈCHES

200ml 6.9 OZ (196 g)

AU BEURRE DE CACAO POUR HYDRATER*

Body Butter by The Body Shop

To moisturize the rest of my body, I usually go for my beloved The Body Shop Body Butter, which smells so delicious I often catch myself nearly giving my arm a bit of a lick

But, really, like most women, I prefer baths to showers, lying in a big sudsy tub, reading some magazines, listening to the radio and getting some time to myself. But with three energetic boys in the house – well, four, really – that's a pretty rare treat. There are so many great bath products out there. I've already mentioned the Laura Mercier range and Kiehl's do really nice special treats too. Space NK's own range of bath salts and tablets is very good value.

A bath is supposed to be a restful, luxurious experience – very old-school Flake advert. But nothing will upset that more if your bathroom itself is looking all messy and cluttered with all of these products lying around. So keep your bath salts and tablets in pretty porcelain jars that you can buy in any second-hand market, particularly Portobello, or from department stores with nice bath departments, such as Liberty's.

For deodorant, I use Nivea Dry Deo Compact, which is a spritzer. Personally, I prefer spritzers, as they leave fewer marks down your top, although, seeing as I always have Johnson's baby wipes on me for emergencies with the kids, I can just wipe those off anyway.

Nivea's hand cream really takes some beating, and Dermalogica's lasts you through the day. Origins makes a good one, the aptly named Make A Difference hand cream, and Bliss's is excellent. To moisturize the rest of my body, I usually go for my beloved The Body Shop Body Butter, which smells so delicious I often catch myself nearly giving my arm a bit of a lick. For a special treat I might sometimes use La Prairie's Skin Caviar Luxe Body Emulsion, which is very expensive but divine. Johnson's baby oil is another good moisturizer but do not use it on the soles of your feet or you'll end up skating across the bathroom floor! Whatever you use, it is important to whack on the body moisturizers as soon as you dry off after your bath or shower since your skin can go very scaly and flaky after getting wet. And remember: moisturizers work best after you've exfoliated as the cream can really get into your skin instead of just sitting on top of all the dry flakes.

If you suffer from puffy eyes, find a good viscous cream or gel (I like La Prairie's, and Dr Harris & Co is excellent too), keep it in the fridge and pat a touch on when needed. It is the coolness that really helps to soothe down the pouches, hence the old technique of relying on cucumber slices and used teabags before a big night out.

For daily moisturizers, I use a combination of products by Dermalogica, Yonka, Re Vive, La Prairie and The Body Shop, depending on what I feel my skin needs at that time. Obviously, I don't use all of the products listed below at once as that would not only really clog my skin but it would also take half the morning to put on! So think of these recommendations as things to pick and choose from according to your skin needs. I was introduced to Yonka by Linda Meredith, whose hugely popular London salon I visit for facials when I'm in town (and incidentally, Linda also has her own great range of skincare products). Yonka products are light enough for my oily skin but I can still feel them working, especially their Firming Treatment Cream. Re Vive is a very good range as well, particularly their Sensitif Oil Free Volumizing Lotion SPF 15, Lip and Perioral Renewal Cream, and Eye Renewal Cream, which is very light so works well for daytime. In the evenings, I'll switch to La Prairie's Cellular Radiance Eye Cream, which is richer and you really need only a dab as otherwise it will look like you've smeared Tippex under your eyes.

If your skin isn't so oily, I think the best daily moisturizers are by a Japanese company called SKII, which you can find in Selfridges, and the Jo Malone range, particularly her Orange and Geranium Moisturizer mixed with the Protein Serum. All of Jo's products are just delicious and smell as lovely and light as her candles. For a real treat, go to one of her stores for a facial – honestly, a friend of mine went and she came back an hour later looking like she'd been on holiday for two weeks. Vaishaly has started doing a skincare range and her night cream in particular is great.

Origins also do good moisturizers for young skin, particularly their A Perfect World skin guardian, which is just a light filmy cream that goes beneath your moisturizer and gives your skin extra protection against daily dirt and grime, and truly does make an enormous difference to your skin. Origins say this is because it is made from white tea, which is supposed to be very good for your skin, even better than green tea, and everyone recommends drinking both to maintain a good complexion. I have to admit, I find this really hard as they are so bitter, but both kinds of tea are now available flavoured with fruits, such as lemon or pineapple, which makes looking after my skin a much more delicious job; though being able to cream it on my face makes it even easier.

Don't forget to moisturize your neck too: this is one of the first things to go and so many people just completely neglect it. Obviously, you can just use your normal moisturizer for this, but high-end ranges now make products especially for the neck as it does have

The most important thing is to protect your skin from the sun . . . Make

different moisturizing needs from your face. For example, La Prairie does a lovely one called Cellular Neck Cream but it is, as La Prairie always is, expensive. And finally, always apply your moisturizer on your neck and face in an upwards motion as that will give you a natural perky flush.

Really, you can spend a squillion pounds on your skin but the most important thing is to protect your skin from the sun. Always make sure that your moisturizer and foundation have an SPF in them, and it doesn't hurt to add some extra sunblock on top, to protect you from the sun's harmful rays all year round.

Picking spots is another bad one. The worst is when you stay in a hotel and it has one of those amazing magnifying mirrors you never see anywhere but in hotels. It's so tempting to peer into it and say, 'Oh, God! I didn't know I had a blackhead there!' And then squeeze it. But, honestly, squeezing really does make it worse and can give you little scars. OK, yeah, I know, it is easy just to say not to squeeze your spots but, really, everybody does it. So if you absolutely must, use your forefingers and a tissue and always make sure you use a good anti-bacterial facewash afterwards as at least this will stop the bacteria spreading. I use Dermalogica's Antibacterial Skin Wash.

But the best things you can do for your skin don't cost a penny: get lots of sleep and drink loads of water – two things, admittedly, I struggle to do myself. But one thing I really want to stress is that looking after your skin is not about trying to hold back the years, despite what some moisturizers claim. Because nothing, and I mean nothing, is going to keep you looking twenty and that is just fine. Looking good is not dependent on looking young. It's about making the best of yourself and feeling good and healthy.

As for facelifts and all the rest of it, well, if it makes you happy, fine. It's up to the individual and, as I said, if it makes you feel more confident, and it's guaranteed to be safe, then go for it, it's your life.

Then for the rest of your body, it's always flattering to have a bit of body shimmer or tinted moisturizer if you're wearing a short dress or skirt or a sleeveless top. Just a slick of something like Nars Body Glow or a tinted body moisturizer by Estée Lauder can make you look healthier, more toned and even out your skin colour.

sure that your moisturizer and foundation have an SPF in them

MAC's Strobe Cream is great too. For quick fake tans, if you can't be bothered with the whole St Tropez thing, there are some fantastic easy fixes around now. Space NK in particular has a really good selection of quick, spray-on, natural-looking tans. And I always prefer spray-on to cream tans as I don't want all that gunk on my hands and to end up looking like I've been Tangoed. Tan Airbrush in a Can by ModelCo is my favourite and a real essential in my bathroom cabinet, and Bronze Airbrush Sun, also by ModelCo, gives a lovely natural tan to your face. For the evening, ModelCo's Shimmer Airbrush Illuminator gives a light tan with just a hint of shimmer, but the best one is probably Body Bling by Scott Barnes, which I stock up on every time I go to the States. Honestly, so many actresses use it when they have to go to red-carpet events because it looks so natural but at the same time makes such a difference, giving you a healthy colour that is so flattering, and it can even make your arms and legs look all toned up. And that reminds me, you should always check out beauty products when you go abroad as you'll find all sorts of cool things that you can't get at home, and different countries are really good for different things. For example, America is great for fake tans and France has good moisturizers.

With make-up, the first thing to ask yourself is whether you're stuck in a beauty rut. If

Shimmer shadow by MAC

*Make-up compacts
by Giorgio Armani*

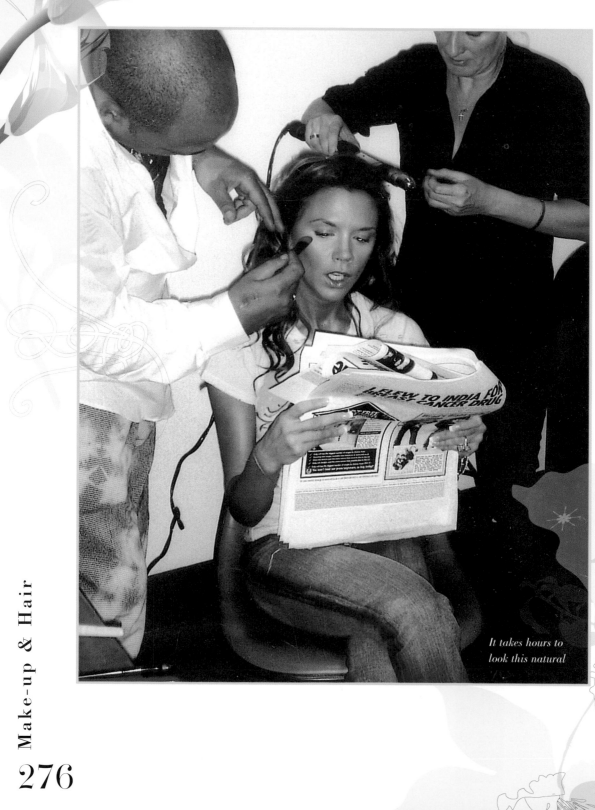

It takes hours to
look this natural

you've been automatically using the same make-up in the same way for the past ten years, then you definitely are and you could look out of date too. Plus, what suited you when you were, say, eighteen, is not going to suit you when you're twenty-eight, as your face will obviously have changed. A lot of people get quite nervous about the idea of changing their make-up, mainly because they feel they just don't know what to do or where to start. Some people recommend going to a department-store beauty hall and getting tips from the sales assistants. Concentrate on what new colours and shades they're putting on your eyes and what new creams they're putting on your face.

Bobbi Brown is great for a subtle, natural look, particularly their tinted powders and shimmery eyeshadows. If you want something more dramatic, MAC is brilliant. The latter company was set up by a professional make-up artist because he couldn't find anything that worked on fashion shoots, so the make-up always comes in fabulous colours and really lasts. I have found that the sales assistants at the MAC make-up counters are very, very good and honest.

But the easiest way of all to get ideas is just to look through the beauty sections of magazines as these are generally pretty reader-friendly and they also have the most up-to date techniques and looks. *Glamour*'s beauty section is always really good and *Vogue* always features the latest products and treatments available.

Also, ask yourself if you have a make-up crutch: you know, a product or look that you rely on too much. Look through photos of yourself over a long period of time and see if you can spot something. Geri used to be really addicted to eyeliner, for example, and, as though she was an alcoholic, we had to wean her off it. Mine is definitely lipliner and I have a real tendency to put on much too much, although I am trying to give up!

One thing I really love about make-up is how you can bond over it with other girls, swapping tips and trying out one another's products. You can spend a lot of money on bits and bobs but, to be honest, there are loads of cheaper ranges around now that are great. Bourjois is very good, especially their pearlized eyeshadows, and Rimmel has really great things too, particularly their mascaras. And there are some products you really can skimp on, such as nail varnish. My favourite brands are Chanel and Nars. But when I run out I often just dash into a supermarket and get a cheap nail polish. Yeah, it might chip quicker but it's perfect if you're just rushing out for the night.

STILA LIPGLOSSES AND THE FAMOUS JUICY TUBES BY LANCÔME ARE GREAT

However, if you do want to spend a bit more on your make-up, I definitely recommend Giorgio Armani. I don't normally wear foundation but Armani foundations are so light anyone can master them, and the colours are really nice and subtle. Other good foundations include Prescriptives' Traceless, which smoothes out your complexion but is just what its name promises, and, if you want something less liquid, Chantecaille's Real Skin is a real favourite of many of the professionals. They're not exactly foundations but a lot of the best beauty brands have started making something called face illuminators, which really help to brighten up your face and give it a bit of a sparkle. Guerlain, Dior and Chanel do good ones, as does Prescriptives. Illuminators give your face a bit of a subtle shimmer and basically make you look very perky even if you've been up half the night with the baby, or possibly for more glamorous reasons.

For colourful make-up, MAC is, for me, one of the best. I love Nars too, especially their

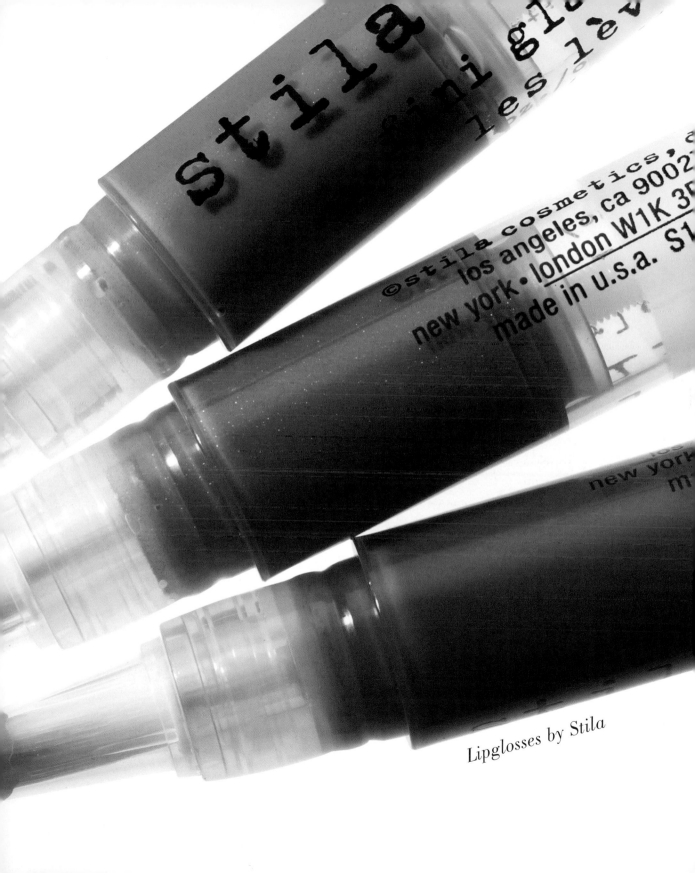

stila
mini gl
les lèv

©stila cosmetics,
los angeles, ca 9002
new york • london W1K 3
made in u.s.a. S1

new york

Lipglosses by Stila

Multiple in Copacabana, which I use on my cheekbones to give them a bit of a lift. Subtle dashes of iridescence really make your face look so youthful and healthy. Chantecaille make some beautiful products, particularly their multi-palettes, which are so amazingly useful: they have a selection of some of the prettiest eyeshadow shades, including one charcoal one that you can use as an eyeliner with a flat, wet brush, and then two different shades of blusher. Stila lipglosses and the famous Juicy Tubes by Lancôme are great but the best are by Versace: they make your lips look really plump but not sticky, and are glittery but not overly so. Plus, the packaging is so brilliant, all fabulous and Versace-like.

That's another thing I love about make-up: it lets you enjoy designer labels and packaging – like me and my Gucci school-satchel carrier bag. It's not about snobbery; it's about being able to enjoy life's luxuries without having to spend a fortune.

And so I do think the packaging of make-up is

Make-up & Hair

281

a bit of a factor when you're deciding what to buy. When I was a kid, a friend of my mum's used to give me her empty Chanel No. 5 bottles, which I would line up on my dressing table, just because I loved looking at them. I still prefer the products to match each other as opposed to just cluttering up the basin with random bits and bobs.

If I'm looking a little tired, I'll then dab on some Touche Eclat by YSL as that is amazing at covering up dark circles, and maybe put in some Optrex eye drops, depending on how bad the situation is. Always curl your lashes – I like Shu Uemura curlers – as that opens your eyes out, and this is doubly true if you're looking a bit puffy and sleepy, and then give them a bit of a comb through with a lash comb to get rid of any potential clumps. Finally, I'll get a quick spritz of Oxygen 81's Oxygen Revitalizing Treatment, which fixes your make-up in place. I'll just chuck some Johnson's baby wipes in my bag with Eight Hour cream, gloss for my lips and maybe some blusher, and I'm set for the day. But, for heaven's sake, before you leave the house, always take a good hard look at yourself in a full-length mirror. It's not a good look to leave the house with your skirt tucked into your knickers and mascara halfway down your face.

Ever since I was collecting empty No. 5 bottles, I've always had a real thing about perfume. Perfume scents can take me back like nothing else: Raffini reminds me of my mum kissing me goodnight before heading out on a Saturday night back in the 80s, wearing shoulder pads and a velvet skirt. Then there's Charlie, Anaïs Anaïs, Joy and Poison, all of which take me back to my childhood too. But because I love perfume so much, I do have very particular rules about how it should be worn. Number one, don't wear too much because it just becomes overpowering instead of

Make-up brushes by MAC and eyelash curlers by Shu Uemura

Another kind of perfume that looks good and smells wonderful is the Miller Harrris range

Perfume by Miller Harris

eau de parfum

Miller Harris

PERFUMER LONDON

subtly seductive, as it's supposed to be. So just dab it on, don't douse it. Just a little dab on the back and sides of the neck and on the inner wrists, as those are the pulse points and emit fragrance best. It's best not to spray any in your hair as this can make your hair go frizzy and funny if you colour it. I prefer light perfumes, as strong ones can give me a headache, and I was really strict about that when David and I were creating our perfume, Intimately with Coty. It was so interesting to learn about the process, seeing how they press the flowers, mix the oils and how the smallest adjustment of the proportions completely alters the scent.

I also really like Marc Jacobs' perfume, which is lovely, very delicate but delicious, and you can now get it in a solid compact, which looks beautiful and also means you can carry it about in your handbag without the threat of spillage. I do love solid perfumes: there is something so charmingly old-fashioned about them and they always look so gorgeous on your dressing table – Estée Lauder does fabulously ornate ones – and, as I said, they are so practical too. Another kind of perfume that looks good and smells wonderful is the Miller Harris range. I particularly like their single-note scents as they are very fresh and light and the bottles, which are chunky and square but painted with delicate flowers, are brilliant. A couple of years ago, Patsy Kensit made me such a kind present of a personalized bottle of perfume from Miller Harris. She told the company what kind of fragrances I like, they mixed up the oils accordingly and it was then presented in the most beautiful bottle engraved with my name. This is, of course, a pretty expensive present, but it is a very, very special one.

If you like clean perfumes, Philosophy do some really nice, young-smelling ones too,

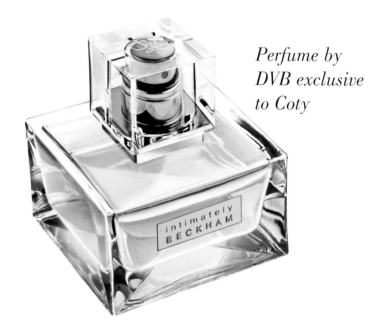

Perfume by DVB exclusive to Coty

in their Grace range, which actually makes you smell as clean and fresh as, well, a baby!

I also love perfumes from Creed, and the bottles look so grand, as if they come from another era. And they almost do: the company was originally set up in 1760 in London, though later moved to Paris, and its perfumes were worn by many members of European royalty. The company has always stayed in the Creed family, which I think is really special, and it still uses traditional perfume-making techniques, something almost no other companies do.

My favourite of their range is Floris, which I love even more ever since finding out that Audrey Hepburn wore it.

Scented oils are also nice to use as perfumes and are often more subtle. Kiehl's musk oil is gorgeous, and Prada have made some pretty floral ones. Again, just dab a touch on your pulse points and you're all set.

I'll tell you something else that you really don't have to spend lots of money on. I wear acrylic nails and I'm always looking for people who can put them on properly as a badly put on nail is not a pleasant thing to see. I've been out in the States and people tell me, 'Oh, you must go see this person, she does so and so's nails, they cost a fortune but they're the best,' and so on. So I go, get them done, pay a ridiculous amount of money and the next day the bloody things fly right off my hand! I think if you find a nail technician that is quick and good, make sure that they are not overcharging and use quality products. I see this amazing Vietnamese man up in north London and I can tell you, he costs a lot less than some of the pricey and overly hyped people I've seen, and his work lasts much, much longer. So you need to find someone good and, contrary to what a lot of people think, good does not always mean expensive.

I wear fake toenails too, because I'm almost always wearing open-toed shoes. There is one situation, though, when having long acrylic nails is not so helpful – changing babies' nappies. I can tell you, you can get some really unpleasant things stuck under your nails then . . .

For nail colour, I recommend either the colour of the season or deep red, which is always a classic

ONE PART OF YOUR BEAUTY ROUTINE THAT IS WORTH SPENDING MONEY ON IS YOUR HAIRCUT AND COLOUR

For nail colour, I recommend either the colour of the season or deep red, which is always a classic, or beige, as that makes your legs and fingers look longer, in the way beige shoes do. It's also not so obvious when the paint chips. And, speaking of chips, always give your nails a topcoat of clear polish to help protect the paint that little bit longer. One of my favourite brands of nail polish is Nars.

Eyebrow threading is another treatment that doesn't have to cost much and makes a real difference. This is an ancient hair-removal technique in which someone twists cotton and uses it to pull out stray hairs around your eyebrows or anywhere on your face. It is much less painful than plucking and the hairs grow back thinner and lighter. As you can imagine, this is a real skill that takes time to learn, but there are increasing numbers of threading salons around, particularly in London. The best known is probably Vaishaly, which is such a blissful spa near Marylebone, and you'll often bump into some surprising people in the waiting room.

One part of your beauty routine that is worth spending money on is your haircut and colour. Yeah, sure, hair always does grow back so it might seem like a lot of money to spend over £50 on something that will need to be done again in six weeks' time, but think about it: this is the very first thing people see when they look at you; it completely affects how you look – more, even, than anything you might wear; and you'll see it every time you look in the mirror. So if anything is worth getting done properly, surely this is it. Ask around before you go to a salon as you'll find that even some of the best-known places are only good for straight hair and others are not so great for short hair, or whatever, and the only way you'll learn is by reliable word of mouth. And while we're on the subject, I've recently cut my hair – it feels great to have a new image, but there's so much more you can do with long hair, if you haven't got the time to wash it you can simply twist it up into a ponytail.

I've been using hair extensions for years, but you really have to go somewhere that knows how to put them in properly. There are so many people walking around with very bad extensions: you can see the glue holding the bonds in at the scalp, the extensions themselves look all frizzy because they're made out of nylon instead of real hair, and the whole thing doesn't look great. Once you have them, you have to look after them carefully and accept that they are quite high-maintenance. First, you need to use a special shampoo and conditioner, something many people mistakenly don't bother about. Next, be careful when you go swimming. Sometimes I see people running into the sea with their hair extensions and it just makes me wince as there is nothing like sea water for making your extensions go all matted; then you have to cut them out, and I know people who've had to have theirs cut out along with their own hair too. If you go swimming in the sea, always tie your hair back very tightly. And finally, don't do what I did and pick at the glue. Not a good look and I was always vowing that I'd stop – tomorrow.

Another high-maintenance hair treatment is highlights, and because they are, I tend to get them done only for special occasions, and maybe sometimes in the summer too. I often get them done for Christmas parties and my hairdresser, Ben Cooke, who runs a salon in London called Lockonego, calls it turning on the Christmas lights! But whenever you get them, always get subtle ones, not those weird zebra stripes; just go for a shade or two lighter than your normal colour.

In terms of daily haircare, if you want a groomed, quite sleek look, like I do, you have to wash your hair every day.

If you have extensions, you need to check that the shampoo doesn't have any oil in it as this can cause the extensions to fall out. Conditioner is fine, but only put it on the mid-length and tips, never the roots of the extensions. Then, after you've rinsed everything out of your hair, give it a blast of cold water as that seals the cuticles and gives your hair a real shiny glossiness. So, as you're standing there, shivering to death in the shower, just repeat to yourself, 'Short-term pain, long-term pleasure, short-term pain, long-term pleasure'.

I always like to go for a natural kind of look

Blonde Ambition

Just remember that looser, but still tidy, hair is sexier and that having horrible helmet hair can make a person look like a fifty-year-old librarian

If your hair is straight, like mine, it can have a tendency to go a little flat. So I often spray some lift onto the roots – I really like the Body Double range by Sebastian, especially the Volumizing Spray. To give your hair a bit more of a lift, comb it through with a wide-toothed comb – one of the best things to use on wet hair – and then finish off with a good blast under the hairdryer. To lift it even more, I'll then really blast it under the hairdryer while hanging my head upside down, until it's about 75 per cent dry, then work through the hair with a wide-paddle natural-bristle brush – Mason Pearson brushes work best with my hair, and most other people's too, I've found. If you have long hair and want to add some texture you can take some large tongs and work them through the whole length of your hair, from root to tip, holding the tips onto the tongs so you get a really nice large-wave effect through your hair.

As you can see, I really don't use many hair products. I hate that feeling of having loads of gunk in my hair, and that first-lady look of having this big immobile helmet of hair is so not me. I want my hair to look quite relaxed, but groomed and clean. At most, I might top off my hair with some Redken products, which are very light, to keep the style a little, but only rarely. Even for big special occasions my hair tends to be quite loose and free – I don't fuss over it too much as it will look all fussy and stiff. Yes, even for big parties you should just give your hairdo a quick once-over and then go. Just remember that looser, but still tidy, hair is sexier and that having horrible helmet hair can make a person look like a fifty-year-old librarian.

THE FIRST FASHION SHOW I EVER WENT TO WAS IN MILAN. IT WAS 1997 AND I WAS STILL VERY MUCH A SPICE GIRL.

WHICH IS WHY WE WERE STUCK IN THIS CHATEAU IN THE SOUTH OF FRANCE REHEARSING – GETTING OUR ACT TOGETHER AS YOU MIGHT SAY – FOR OUR FIRST EVER STADIUM SHOW.

For six weeks we had had no social life at all – so suddenly finding myself in the front row of one of the most prestigious catwalk shows in the world felt as magical (and unlikely) as Cinderella finding herself at the ball. My fairy godmother was Donatella Versace, who invited me not only to the show itself but to the party afterwards, and then to stay the night at her amazing palazzo on Lake Como. Of course, Cinderella Spice could hardly turn up in her little black Miss Selfridge dress – nice as it was – but Donatella had thought of everything and waved her wand in the direction of the Versace shop, and I can still remember the thrill of being let loose and told I could choose whatever I wanted. I honestly thought it was a once-in-a-lifetime experience and, of course, in many ways it was. But this was the first time I had ever been that close to the fashion world, and it was like the fuse of a firework had been lit.

Eight years down the line, Roberto Cavalli invited me to actually be in his show. After being a spectator for so long I was unbelievably nervous, terrified I would do something really stupid, like trip over. In fact, every model has that fear – however many times they've done it before – knowing that with one false move they'll end up on the front page, and not for the right reasons. They joked that at least I wouldn't have far to fall. And it was true that, even when I was wearing my highest heels, the girls towered above me.

Milano - Dolce & Gabbana
SHow 9·30·2001

Fo,
Victoria

R. Toledo

What you never see when you're sitting out front, is what the models put on once the runway clothes are handed back. Naturally they all have their individuality but one thing remains the same: they have bags of style, but keep it simple. Which brings me back to Cinderella. If you have ever seen a production of the pantomime, you will know that the biggest laughs come from the Ugly Sisters – or rather from what they are wearing. It's the annual opportunity for everyone to poke fun at fashion. Obviously the fashions concerned are exaggerated, but what the pantomime does show is the thin line between trying too hard and total hilarity. Trendy and cool are not the same thing.

The moment you stand in front of that mirror and feel those little questions creeping in – Is this really me? Could I be a walking inspiration for an Ugly Sister? – then it's time to think again.

I'm not saying you should never take risks, far from it, because fashion is one of the few areas of your life where you don't have to conform to other people's ideas about who you are. It's where you can truly show your individuality. The trick is to find the balance, to wear what works for your individual body shape while at the same time keeping track of what's happening in the fashion world, to ensure you don't get stuck in a rut. Have you ever noticed how some older women can look as if they're in a time warp? It's what I call the security-blanket style of dressing. Just because something suited you once doesn't mean you have to go on wearing it for ever. In the same way that fashion moves on, so should you.

The easiest way of keeping up with fashion trends is by keeping tabs on the heart of the industry, the collections. In the old days the shows were kept strictly under wraps. Cameras weren't allowed in and journalists could only do sketches. Now there are as many photographers as spectators and it's easy to pick up all you need to know from fashion magazines or, best of all, online at www.style.com.

Photographs taken on the catwalk are great for showing you how to wear the looks – for preparing you for that moment six months later when you're in the shop, standing in front of the mirror, thinking: I like it, but what have I got to go with it?

Because of the way the fashion year is structured, there's plenty of time to digest the ideas before the clothes become available in the shops. However glamorous they might appear, the collections are basically trade shows, and the clothes on the catwalk are the samples. If the buyers don't like what they see (and most of the people sitting alongside the runways are buyers, not celebrities) they won't put in their orders and the clothes won't get made. It's that simple.

Make that delay work for you. There are some trends that take time to get used to. Take shorts. Until very recently they were strictly for holidays or lap dancers. It was only when they began appearing on the runway that their full fashion potential was realized, and the moment they arrived in Topshop they walked out of the door – as if everyone was making up for all those lost summers in the city.

As somebody once said, time spent in research is never wasted, and this is particularly true in fashion. Although designer pieces are usually outside the price range of girls in their teens or early twenties, the collections are still a great place to look for inspiration and for spotting trends. Among the younger designers I would include Marc Jacobs, Marc by Marc Jacobs, Miu Miu, Chloe and Stella McCartney. Shows are also the time when fashion writers really get an opportunity to flex their muscles; their take may not always be your take, but they can give you the history of where a particular look has its origins, the way it can translate from the runway to everyday life.

That first time I went to Milan, I felt as out of place as a shell suit in a couture showroom. But over the last ten years, both as a consumer and now as a designer myself, I have felt increasingly comfortable, having discovered that the fashion world is not the intimidating place I once imagined it to be. And I can honestly say that some of the nicest people I have ever met work in the industry. Fashion is like anything else: the more you know, the less scary it is.

My attitude to fashion is pure *Sex and the City* – as the millions of girls who fell under Carrie Bradshaw's spell will recognize. She didn't blindly follow trends; the way she put together her own outfits was totally original and fabulous. Like herself: beautiful, but in an unconventional way. Of course, Sarah Jessica Parker and her stylists on the show brought in new fun pieces, and would work them into the existing wardrobe rather than chucking everything out and starting again. If you looked carefully you could see that it was based on gorgeous classics, sexy pencil dresses and amazing accessories, like the perfect Manolos. They simply gave them their own spin. Best of all, Carrie dressed for herself: she knew that she looked great and she was having fun. Who cared that some of her boyfriends didn't get it? In other words, she was a girls' girl and that is really why women so fell for her.

'I've known Victoria since she married David and I saw her growing with a very special style that today has inspired millions of girls. I like her way of working with accessories to make a dress become more special'

VALENTINO

Of course, it takes time to build up the confidence to carry this off, and it's particularly hard when you're a teenager and all you want to do is fit in. Sometimes it seems easiest to just follow the trends or make yourself look older. Don't do it. Don't listen to the voices that say you have to look a certain way. Fashion is about looking like you. Make a good foundation, then add those little details to bring it up to date. For twenty-somethings, feminine and cool looks best, such as little white T-shirts under dresses. For thirty-somethings, cut back on the make-up, and try experimenting with dress and skirt shapes you wouldn't have even noticed a year or two back, like the way I've got so much more into pencil skirts recently. When I was in the Spice Girls, I probably wouldn't have even spotted them on the rails; all I saw were teeny miniskirts. These kinds of changes are not a sign that you're starting to dress frumpily: they are a sign that you are getting to know what looks best on you.

If I could go back in time, I would tell my teenage self to have more confidence about these things, as that was one thing I definitely lacked.

No one knows better than you what makes you feel good about yourself and look fantastic. So take a deep breath, keep your head up and just walk down that catwalk . . .

When I go out now, I dress first for myself, then for David and then for my girlfriends. Knowing that the people I care about like how I look gives me more confidence than anything else ever could. If you feel particularly good about yourself in something, or someone important in your life makes a nice comment about it, you will always associate that outfit with that moment, and that's why clothes work almost like a scrapbook of your life. At least they do for me, which is one reason why I have kept virtually everything I've ever worn, from the little black Miss Selfridge dress from the Spice Girls' days and the brown suede dress I wore on one of my first dates with David, to the Cavalli Ming Vase print dress I wore to Elton's ball, made all the more special to me because David picked it out. And every time I look at those clothes, they bring back the memories that they hold, and I smile.

If there's one thing I hope you take away from this book, it's that fashion is brilliant, brilliant fun, and the knowledge that something's working for you will have you walking on air every time you leave the house. And if you're happy with the way you look, then this will communicate itself to everyone you meet.

The day I did the Roberto Cavalli show in Milan, I was so petrified of falling over in front of the whole fashion world, that I did what every girl does when she's running scared. I rang my mum. 'Victoria,' she said, 'you've been walking for thirty-one bloody years, you should have mastered it by now!' And she was absolutely right. I didn't fall over, and I had a brilliant time.

So that's what I would like to say to all of you: listen to your inner voice, not to the comments other people might make. No one knows better than you what makes you feel good about yourself and look fantastic. So take a deep breath, keep your head up and just walk down that catwalk.

WHERE TO BUY

9 LONDON 020 7352 7600
www.9london.co.uk
10 CORSO COMO 10 Corso Como
00 (39) 2 654 831
www.10corsocomo.com
ABERCROMBIE & FITCH
for mail order to the UK:
www.abercrombie.com
ACCESSORIZE 0870 412 9000
www.accessorize.co.uk
ACNE JEANS 00 1 212 414 5814
www.acnejeans.com
ADIDAS 0870 240 4204
www.adidas.com
AGATHA 4 South Molton St, W1;
enq & mail order 020 7495 2779
AGENT PROVOCATEUR 0870 600
0229 www.agentprovocateur.com
AGNÈS B 01865 790 799
www.agnesb.com
ALEX GORE BROWNE
020 7419 1200
www.alexgorebrowne.com
ALEXANDER MCQUEEN
20 7278 4333
www.alexandermcqueen.com
ALL SAINTS enq 0870 428 3500;
www.allsaints.co.uk
ALTERNA www.4alterna.com
AMERICAN APPAREL
020 7734 4477
www.americanapparel.net
ANGELS 020 8202 2244
www.angels.uk.com
ANNA SUI available at Fenwicks
0207 629 9161, The Cross 0207 727
6760, www.netaporter.com
www.annasui.com
ANNA MOLINARI
www.annamolinari.net
ANYA HINDMARCH
020 7501 0177
www.anyahindmarch.com
APC Aime, 32 Ledbury Rd, W11; enq
020 7221 7070; enq in Paris
(00 33 1) 4987 0404; www.apc.fr
ARMANI 020 7235 6263/020 7318
2486 www.armani.com
AROMATHERAPY ASSOCIATES

www.aromatherapyassociates.com
ASPREY 020 7493 6767
www.asprey.com
AUSSIE www.aussiehair.com
AVEDA 01730 232 380
www.aveda.com
AZZEDINE ALAÏA available at
Browns, Liberty and Selfridges
BABY DIOR Dior, 31 Sloane St,
SW1; enq 020 7172 0172;
www.dior.com
BALENCIAGA stocked by Harrods,
Harvey Nichols and Selfridges
www.balenciaga.com
BARNEYS 001 888 222 7639
www.barneys.com
BATHING APE www.bape.com
BELLA FREUD 020 8969
25180www.bellafreud.co.uk
BELLE & BUNTY
enq 020 7267 3322;
www.belleandbunty.co.uk
BERTIE 020 7380 5800
BETTY JACKSON 020 7589 7884
www.bettyjackson.com
BEYOND RETRO 020 7613 3636
www.beyondretro.com
BLAKES available at
www.net-a-porter.com
BLISS 0808 100 4151
www.blisslondon.co.uk
BLOOMIN MARVELLOUS
0845 458 7408
www.bloominmarvellous.co.uk
BLOSSOM MOTHER & CHILD
020 7589 7500
www.blossommotherandchild.com
BLUE CULT www.bluecult.com
BOBBI BROWN available at
Fenwick, House of Fraser and
Selfridges
BONDS OF AUSTRALIA
www.bondsaustralia.co.uk
BONPOINT 001 212 879 0900
www.bonpoint.com
BOOTS 0845 070 8090
www.boots.co.uk
THE BODY SHOP
01903 844 554

BOTTEGA VENETA 020 7838 9394
www.bottegaventa.com
THE BUTTON SHOP
www.button-shop.com
THE BUTTON QUEEN
020 7935 1505
www.thebuttonqueen.co.uk
BOURJOIS www.bourjois.com
available at pharmacies nationwide
BRORA 0207 736 9944
www.brora.co.uk
BROWNS 020 7514 0000
www.brownsfashion.com
BROWNS FOCUS 020 7514 0063
(website address as above)
BURBERRY enq 07000 785 676;
www.burberry.com
BUTLER & WILSON 020 7409 2955
www.butlerandwilson.co.uk
C&C CALIFORNIA available at
Browns, The Cross, Liberty, Harvey
Nichols and Selfridges
www.candccalifornia.com
CACHAREL 020 7383 3000 available
at www.net-a-porter.com
CALVIN KLEIN UNDERWEAR enq
020 7290 5900; www.cku.com
CAMDEN MARKET
www.camdenlock.net
CAROLINA HERRERA
www.carolinaherrera.com
CATH KIDSTON 020 7229 8000
www.cathkidston.co.uk
CHANEL 26 Old Bond St, W1;
enq 020 7493 5040; www.chanel.com
CHANTECAILLE 020 7629 9161
available at Fenwick and Space NK
CHANTILLY www.chantilly.co.uk
CHERRY CHAU available at
Harvey Nichols
CHLOE 020 7823 5348 www.chloe.com
CHRISTIAN DIOR 020 7172 0172
www.fashiondior.com
CHRISTIAN LOUBOUTIN
020 7245 6510 also available at
www.net-a-porter.com
CITIZENS OF HUMANITY stocked
by Harvey Nichols, selected House of
Fraser stores and Selfridges

CLAIRE'S ACCESSORIES
www.claires.co.uk
CLARINS 0800 036 3558
COCO RIBBON 21 Kensington Park
Rd, W11; enq 020 7229 4904; 133
Sloane St, SW1; enq 020 7730 8555;
www.cocoribbon.com
COLETTE 00 33 1 55 35 33 90
www.colette.fr
COLLONIL 00 49 0 30 414 04511
www.collonil.com
CONNECT HAIR SYSTEM
020 7483 3845
COWSHED PRODUCTS
020 7851 1173
www.cowshedproducts.com
CREED available at Harrods
020 7730 1234
CRÈME DE LA MER 01730 232 566
www.cremedelamer.com
DAMARIS available at
www.becheeky.com
DAY BIRGER et MIKKELSON
 020 7432 8088 www.day.dk
DE GRISOGONO
www.degrisogono.com
DECADES www.decadesvintage.com
DENTS 01985 212 291
www.dents.co.uk
DERMALOGICA 0800 591 818
www.dermatalogica.com
DIANE VON FURSTENBURG
83 Ledbury Rd, W11; enq 020 7221
1120; www.dvflondon.com
DIDIER LUDOT 331 42 96 06 56
www.didierludot.com
DIOR SUNGLASSES 020 8415 999
DIPTYQUE 020 7201 0989
DIVERSE 020 7359 8877
DOLCE AND GABBANA 020 7201
0989 www.dolcegabbana.it
DONNA KARAN 19 New Bond St,
W1S; 020 7495 3100;
www.donnakaran.com
DOVE 0800 085 1548 www.dove.com
available at pharmacies nationwide
DR HARRIS & CO 020 7930 3915
www.drharris.co.uk
DSQUARED 020 7600 4841
www.dsquared2.com
EARNEST SEWN 020 7713 9392
www.earnestsewn.com
ELEMIS 01278 727 830
www.elemis.co.uk
ELEY KISHIMOTO

www.eleykishimoto.com
ELIZABETH ARDEN 0870 034 5622
www.elizabetharden.com
ELLA MOSS 020 7713 9392
www.ellamoss.com
ELLE MACPHERSON INTIMATES
020 7478 0280
www.ellemacphersonintimates.com
ELSPETH GIBSON available to
order 020 7235 0601
www.elspethgibson.com
EMANUEL UNGARO 020 7629 0550
ERICKSON BEAMON 020 7259 0202
www.ericksonbeamon.co.uk
ESTÉE LAUDER 01730 232 566
www.esteelauder.co.uk
FAITH 0800 289 297 www.faith.co.uk
FALKE 020 7493 8442
FENDI 22 Sloane St, SW1;
Selfridges, W1; enq 020 7838 6288;
www.fendi.com
FENWICK 020 7629 9161
www.fenwick.co.uk
FIFI CHACHNIL
www.fifichachnil.com also available
at www.redoute.co.uk
FLORENCE + FRED 0800 505 555
www.clothingattesco.com
FOGAL 020 7235 3115 www.fogal.com
FORNICA available at Harrods
www.fornica.com
FRANKIE B 001 213 624 5411
www.frankieb.com
FREEDOM @ TOPSHOP 01277 844
186 www.freedomjewellery.co.uk
FRENCH CONNECTION 020 7399
7200 www.frenchconnection.com
FRYE www.fryeboots.com
GAP 0800 427 789 www.gap.com
GEORGE AT ASDA 0500 100 055
www.george.com
GEORGINA GOODMAN 020 8605
3660 www.georginagoodman.com
GHOST 020 7229 1057
www.ghost.co.uk
GOLD SIGN available at
www.revolveclothing.com
GRASS LOS ANGELES
www.grassla.com
THE GREEN ROOM 020 8940 4073
www.thegreen-room.co.uk
GUCCI 34 Old Bond St, W1; enq 020
7629 2716; www.gucci.com
GUERLAIN 01932 233 909
www.guerlain.com

GIUSEPPE ZANOTTI DESIGN
www.giuseppe-zanotti-design.com
H&M enq 020 7323 2211;
www.hm.com
HABITAT 0845 601 0740
www.habitat.net
HABITUAL 001 212 925 9700
www.habitual.com
HARRODS 020 7730 1234
www.harrods.com
HARVEY NICHOLS 020 7235 5000
www.harveynichols.com
HAVAIANAS available at branches of
Office nationwide; www.office.co.uk
HEAD & SHOULDERS
www.headandshoulders.com available
at pharmacies nationwide
HEIDI KLEIN 020 7243 5665
www.heidiklein.co.uk
HERMES 020 7499 8856
www.hermes.com
HOBBS 020 7586 5550
www.hobbs.co.uk
HOSTEL COSTES
00 33 1 42 44 50 00
www.hotelcostes.com
ISSA available at Blossom Mother &
Child 020 7589 7500
JACOB & CO 001 212 719 5887
www.jacobandco.com
JAEGER 01553 732 102
www.jaeger.co.uk
JAMES PERSE www.jamesperse.com
JASPER CONRAN 020 7292 9080
www.jasperconran.com
JD SPORTS 0870 873 0300
www.jdsports.co.uk
JEAN PAUL GAULTIER 020 7584
4648 www.jeanpaul-gaultier.com
JEFFREY 001 212 206 1272
JIMMY CHOO 27 New Bond St, W1;
enq 020 7493 5858; www.net-a-
porter.com
JO MALONE 0870 034 2411
www.jomalone.co.uk
JOE'S JEANS www.joesjeans.com
JOHN LEWIS 08456 049 049
www.johnlewis.com
JOHNNY LOVES ROSIE 020 7247
1496 www.johnnylovesrosie.co.uk
JONATHAN ASTON 01277 204 744
JONELLE exclusive to John Lewis
08456 049 049
JUICY COUTURE available at
Harvey Nichols 020 7235 5000

www.juicycouture.com
JULIEN MACDONALD stocked at
Harrods and Selfridges
JUNGLE 020 7379 5379
www.junglehardwear.com
KAREN MILLEN 0870 160 031
www.karenmillen.com
KAREN WALKER
www.karenwalker.com
KATE SPADE www.katespade.com
KIEHLS 020 7240 2411
www.kiehls.com
KOOKAI www.kookai.co.uk
KURT GEIGER FASHIONISTAS 65
South Molton St, W1; Selfridges, W1;
Harrods, SW1; enq 0845 257 2571;
www.kurtgeiger.com
LA PERLA 020 7291 0930
www.laperla.com
LA PRAIRIE 01932 827 060 available
at House of Fraser 020 7963 2000
LA REDOUTE 0870 0500 455
www.redoute.co.uk
LANCÔME www.lancome.co.uk
LANDS' END 0800 376 7974
www.landsend.co.uk
LANVIN stocked at Harvey Nichols
LAURA MERCIER available at
Harrods, Harvey Nichols, House of
Fraser, Liberty and Space NK 020
7299 4999 www.lauramercier.com
LAURENCE CORNER 020 7813 1010
LEVI'S enq 01604 599752;
www.eu.levi.com
LIBERTY 020 7734 1234
www.liberty.co.uk
LINDA FARROW Harrods, SW1;
enq 020 7730 1234; enq 020 7713
1105; www.lindafarrowvintage.com
LINDA MEREDITH 020 7225 2755
www.lindameredith.com
LINEA AT HOUSE OF FRASER
www.houseoffraser.co.uk
LK BENNETT enq 020 7637 6731;
www.lkbennett.com
LOCKONEGO 020 7795 1798
www.lockonego.com
LOUIS VUITTON 020 7399 4050
www.louisvuitton.com
LOUISE GALVIN 020 7289 5131
www.louisegalvin.com
LOWRY HOTEL AND SPA 0161 827
4000 www.thelowryhotel.com
LUELLA 020 8963 2978
www.luella.com

LULU GUINNESS 020 8483 3333
www.luluguinness.com
MAC 020 7534 9222
www.maccosmetics.co.uk
MAMMA MIA www.blisslondon.co.uk
MANGO 020 7434 3694
www.mangoshops.com
MANOLO BLAHNIK 020 7352 8622
MARC JACOBS AND MARC BY
MARC JACOBS 0800 652 7661
www.marcjacobs.com
MARIA LUISA 00 33 1 470 34808
MARKS & SPENCER enq 0845 302
1234; www.marksandspencer.com
MARNI 020 7245 9520
www.marni.com
MASON PEARSON
www.masonpearson.co.uk
MATALAN www.matalan.co.uk
MATCHES 020 7221 0255
www.matches.co.uk
MATTHEW WILLIAMSON 020 7629
6200 www.matthewwilliamson.com
MIKEY www.mikeyjewellery.com
available at Topshop London flagship store
MILLER HARRIS 020 7629 7750
www.millerharris.com
MISS SELFRIDGE 0800 915 9900
www.missselfridge.co.uk
MISS SIXTY 0870 751 6040
www.misssixty.com
MISSONI 020 7352 2400
www.missoni.com
MIU MIU at www.net-a-porter.com
MODELCO available at Space NK
020 7299 4999 www.modelco.com
MONSOON 020 7313 3000
www.monsoon.co.uk
MOTHERCARE 08453 304030
www.mothercare.com
MULBERRY 41-42 New Bond St,
W1; enq 020 7491 3900;
www.mulberry.com
MYLA 77 Lonsdale Rd, W11, 166
Walton St, SW3; enq 08707 455003;
www.myla.com
NANETTE LEPORE
www.nanettelepore.com
NARS available at Liberty 020 7734
1234 and Space NK 020 7229 4999
www.narscosmetics.com
NEW LOOK 01305 765000
www.newlook.co.uk
NEXT 0845 600 7000 www.next.co.uk
NIKE 0800 056 1640 www.nike.com

NIVEA 0800 616 977 www.nivea.com
available from pharmacies nationwide
NO ADDED SUGAR 020 7226 2223
www.noaddedsugar.co.uk
NORTH FACE 020 7240 9577
www.thenorthface.com
OASIS 01865 881 986
www.oasis-stores.com
OFFICE 0845 580 777
www.office.co.uk
OLD SPITALFIELDS MARKET
www.visitspitalfields.co.uk
www.spitalfields.org.uk
ONE OF A KIND 020 7792 5284
OPTREX www.optrexeyes.com
available from pharmacies nationwide
ORLA KIELY 020 7585 3322
www.orlakiely.com
ORIGINS 0800 731 4039
www.origins.co.uk
ORSINI 020 7937 2903
www.orsini-vintage.co.uk
OXFAM 0845 3000 311
www.oxfam.org
PATRICIA FIELD 001 212 966 4066
www.patriciafield.com
PATRICK COX 020 7730 8886
www.patrickcox.co.uk
PAUL & JOE 39 Ledbury Rd, W11;
enq 020 7243 5510;
www.paul-joe-beaute.com
PEACOCKS 02920 270 000
www.peacocks.co.uk
PEPE 020 7439 0523
www.pepejeans.com
PETIT BATEAU 62 South Molton St,
W1; enq 020 7838 0818;
www.petit-bateau.com
PLAYTEX available at
www.figleaves.com
PPQ 020 7033 3400
www.pqclothing.com
PHILIP TREACY 020 7730 3992
www.philiptreacy.co.uk
PHILLIP LIM www.net-a-porter.com
PHILOSOPHY www.spacenk.com
PHILOSOPHY DI ALBERTA
FERRETTI www.net-a-porter.com
PIED A TERRE www.piedaterre.com
PISTOL PANTIES 75 Westbourne
Park Road, W2; enq 020 7229 5286;
www.pistolpanties.com
POLO RALPH LAUREN
www.polo.com
PORTOBELLO ROAD MARKET

www.portobelloroad.co.uk
PRADA 020 7647 5000
www.prada.com
PRESCRIPTIVES 01730 232 566
www.prescriptives.com
PRESS CLOTHING
www.pressclothing.com
PRINCIPLES www.principles.co.uk
PRINGLE 0800 360 200
www.pringle-clothes.co.uk
PRIMARK 0118 160 6300
www.primark.co.uk
PUCCI 020 7201 8171
www.emiliopucci.com
PURE www.purecollection.com
RADCLIFFE Selfridges, W1; 08/08
377 377; www.radcliffedenim.com
RADIO DAYS 020 7928 0800
www.radiodaysvintage.co.uk
RAY BAN 020 89555 0770
REDKEN available at
www.salonskincare.co.uk
REISS enq 020 7473 9630;
www.reiss.co.uk
RESURRECTION 001 323 651 5516
www.resurrectionvintage.com
REVIVE 0800 085 2716
www.reviveskincare.com
RIGBY AND PELLER 020 7491 2200
www.rigbyandpeller.com
RIMMEL 0845 070 8090
www.rimmellondon.com
ROBERTO CAVALLI 020 7878 8600
www.robertocavalli.net
ROCK AND REPUBLIC Harvey
Nichols, SW1; Harrods, SW1;
enq 020 7734 2039;
www.rockandrepublic.com
ROKIT 020 8801 8600
www.rokit.co.uk
ROLAND MOURET 020 7376 5762
available at www.net-a-porter.com
ROLEX www.rolex.com
RUSSELL AND BROMLEY 020 7629
6903 www.russellandbromley.co.uk
SAMANTHA THAVASA
www.samantha.co.jp
SARA BERMAN enq 020 7485 1425;
www.saraberman.com
SEE BY CHLOE at www.net-a-
porter.com
SASS AND BIDE
www.sassandbide.com available at
Browns Focus, Harvey Nichols and
www.net-a-porter.com

SCOOP 001 212 929 1244
www.scoopnyc.com
SCOTT BARNES 01273 408 800
www.scottbarnes.com
SCREAMING MIMI 001 212 677 6464
www.screamingmimis.com
SEBASTIAN
www.sebastianprofessional.com
SELFRIDGES 0870 837 7377
www.selfridges.com
SERFONTAINE
www.serfontaine.com
7 FOR ALL MANKIND
www.7forallmankind.co
SHELLY'S 020 7437 0452
SHU UEMURA 020 7235 2375
SK-11 0800 072 1771 www.sk2.co.uk
SLATKIN www.slatkin.com
SMYTHSON 020 7318 1515
www.smythson.com
SONIA RYKIEL 020 7493 5255
www.sonialrykiel.com
SOUVENIR 020 7287 8708
SPACE NK 020 7299 4999
www.spacenk.co.uk
SPITFIRE contact@spitfire-design.com,
Also available at Portobello market.
START 020 7729 3334
www.start-london.com
STEINBERG AND TOLKIEN 020
7376 3660
STELLA MCCARTNEY 020 7518
3100 www.stellamccartney.com
STELLA MCCARTNEY
SUNGLASSES 020 7841 5999
STILA 01730 232 566
www.stilacosmetics.com
STRIP 020 7727 2754
www.2strip.com
ST TROPEZ 0115 983 6363
STYLE.COM www.style.com
SUPERFINE Matches, 60-64
Ledbury Rd, W11; enq 020 7221
0255; gen enq 020 7608 9100;
www.superfinelondon.com
SWEATYBETTY 0800 169 3889
www.sweatybetty.com
THOMAS PINK 020 7498 3882
www.thomaspink.co.uk
TIFFANY & CO 020 7499 4577
www.tiffany.com
TIMBERLAND 020 7240 4484
www.timberland.com
TIMPSONS www.timpsons.com
TOAST 0870 220 0460

www.toast.co.uk
TOMAS MAIER 001 888 373 0707
www.tomasmaier.com
TOPSHOP enq 0845 121 4519;
www.topshop.co.uk
TRISH MCEVOY 020 7235 5000
TSUBI available at Browns
TU AT SAINSBUR'S 0800 636 262
www.sainsburys.co.uk
TUMI 0800 783 6570 www.tumi.com
TWEEZERMAN 020 7237 1007
URBAN OUTFITTERS 020 7907
0815 www.urbanoutfitter.co.uk
VAISHALY 020 7224 6088
www.vaishaly.com
VALENTINO 020 7235 5855
www.valentino.it
VANESSA BRUNO available at
www.net-a-porter.com
VBH available at Browns
VELVET 01707 645 828
VELVET (BOUTIQUE) 01282 699 797
VERA WANG www.verawang.com
VERSACE 020 7355 2700
www.versace.com
VERSACE BEAUTY 01273 408 800
VIKTOR & ROLF stocked at selected
Joseph stores www.viktor-rolf.com
VICTORIA'S SECRET 001 937 438
4200 www.victoriassecret.com
VIRGINIA 020 7727 9908
VIVIENNE WESTWOOD 020 7924
4747 www.viviennewestwood.com
WAREHOUSE 0870 122 8813
www.warehouse.co.uk
WHAT GOES AROUND COMES
AROUND 001 212 313 9303
www.myvintage.com
THE WEST VILLAGE 020 7243 6916
Whistles 0870 770 4301
www.whistles.co.uk
THE WHITE COMPANY 01865 881
986 www.thewhitecompany.com
WORN BY www.wornby.co.uk
WOLFORD 020 7499 2549
www.wolfordboutiquelondon.co
WRANGLER available at Topshop
and Urban Outfitter
www.wrangler.co.uk
YSL BEAUTE 01444 255 700
YSL SUNGLASSES 020 7841 5999
YVES SAINT LAURENT 020 7235 6706
YONKA www.yonka.com
ZARA 020 7534 9500 www.zara.com
ZARA HOME www.zarahome.com

Where To Buy

PICTURE SOURCES

Photo on p.17 provided by Western Grove Works, makers of Silver and 1921 brands, from their archives, *circa* 1921. Victoria Beckham in red Roland Mouret dress on p.97. Used by kind permission of Roland Mouret and Richard Young/Rex Features. Victoria Beckham in yellow Robert Cavalli dress on p.138 © Rex Features. Victoria Beckham in Roberto Cavalli Ming Vase dress on p.139 © Kevin Mazur/Wireimage.com. Original sketches on pp.138/139 by Roberto Cavalli. All photos of Victoria Beckham on p.154. Used by kind permission of Tony and Jackie Adams. Manolo Blahnik sketch on pp.156/157. Courtesy of Manolo Blahnik. Victoria Beckham, Manchester Airport, wearing brown poncho, Dec 2004 on p.211 © Matthew Pover/matrixphotos.com. Victoria Beckham, Beverly Hills, wearing a blue poncho, Oct 2004 on p.211 © bigpicturesphoto.com. All pictures of Victoria Beckham on p.243. Used by kind permission of Charlotte Martin. Picture of Victoria Beckham on p.248. Courtesy of David Beckham. Azzedine Alaïa sketch on p.249. Courtesy of Azzedine Alaïa. Artwork on p.298 © Ruben Toledos, 2001. Pictures of Victoria Beckham on p.129, p.135, p.138, p.280, p.291. Used by kind permission of Ben Cooke. Pictures of Victoria Beckham on endpapers. Used by kind permission of Ellen Von Unwerth, Ben Cooke, Charlotte Martin, David Beckham and Andre J. at Patricia Field.

TEXT SOURCES

A special thank you to Manolo Blahnik, Roberto Cavalli, Roland Mouret, Valentino, Matthew Williamson and Christopher Bailey for providing quotes for the book.

WITH THANKS TO . . .

PENGUIN BOOKS: It was so brilliant to be back working with the same team as for my first book, *Learning to Fly*. You have all been amazing and have put up with my perfectionist streak that drives everyone else around me wild. So a big thank you to all: Tom Weldon, Louise Moore, Chantal Gibbs, Katy Follain, John Hamilton, Sophie Brewer, Clare Pollock, Claire Phillips, Claire Bord, Naomi Fidler, Genevieve Shore, Sarah Hulbert, Clare Parkinson, Catherine Hammond, Margaret Bluman, Liz Smith, Rob Williams, Amanda Gooch and all the different departments who have worked so hard to turn this book from a glint in my eye to the sparkling finished product that I am so proud of. And to Nikki Dupin, a special thank you for your brilliant design.

HADLEY FREEMAN: I have long been an admirer of your edgy take on fashion, and what we have both brought to this book is what's made it what it is. Thank you.

JO BURSTON: Without you, Jo, I'd be all over the place. Thank you keeping me on track, and just being there. Not only for me, but David as well. We both really appreciate everything you do for us.

MELISSA ENRILE: Your friendship and help in Madrid has been invaluable to me.

ALL AT 19 ENTERTAINMENT: Catri Drummond, Wendy Edwards, Niki Turner, Charlotte Martin, Sarah Farrow, Sarah Best, Lucy Smith, Ali Parry, Zach Duane and Ceara Redmond. Heartfelt thanks to Nez Gebreel and Maya Maraj for your passion and commitment. Nez, you are my number one partner in crime, and Maya, you laid down your life for this book and that's meant a lot to me.

AND OF COURSE SIMON FULLER: Otherwise known as Mr Make-It-Happen. You have taken my sometimes crazy creative ideas and turned them into business reality. These last few years have not been easy. Thank you for being there for me and David. You are my rock.

ANDREW THOMPSON AND MARK ASHELFORD: (The grim reapers.) Who said lawyers don't have a sense of humour? Thank you for everything.

JULIAN HENRY AND JO MILLOY FOR PUBLICITY: Jo, you had a life before you met me! Joking aside, thank you for your hard work and friendship.

Huge thanks to everybody involved in the photography for this book and whose work in these pages is proof that there's more to me than simply a moody bitch with a pout (otherwise known as the VB paparazzi special).

THE MADRID SHOOT: The wonderful Ellen Von Unwerth and her crew. D & V Management, especially Lawrence Vuillemin, Victoria Adcock, Liz Pugh, Ben Cooke and all at Candia, the invaluable Spanish production team.

THE LONDON SHOOT: Benoît Audureau for photography, Sairey Stemp, Sarah Joan Ross, Jasmine Hennessy from MOT models and all at Size Creative.

BEN COOKE AND MARIA LOUISE FEATHERSTONE – MY CLOSEST FRIENDS: Thank you for all your help and honesty. Maria Louise, in 1982 that Naf-Naf jumper of yours had me green with envy on our first skiing holiday together and it started an avalanche which is still rolling. Thank you for everything.

THE GIRLS: Otherwise known as Geri, Emma, Melanie C and Melanie B. You recognized the person who was there underneath, but who I couldn't see, and gave me the confidence to be myself and not to follow the herd. You put me in the position to write this book. I can never thank you enough.

As for those glittering names I have been privileged to work closely with over the years, I could start at the beginning of the alphabet and work through...but there just isn't the space, so I will limit myself here to those who have not only been an inspiration but generously given me their time: Azzedine Alaïa, Manolo Blahnik, Christopher Bailey, Roberto Cavalli, Roland Mouret, Dolce & Gabbana, Valentino and Matthew Williamson. And behind each one of them there are a dozen others who make it happen. A real heartfelt thank you to you all.

FINALLY, MY FAMILY: Louise, my chief high-street scout for this book – hard work, I know, but fun, you'll have to admit. Mostly I'd like to thank you for your honesty. I might not always have taken it well (I am your big sister after all) but I appreciate it, and please never stop. I love you.
Jackie, Tony and my brother Christian: it's not been easy over the past few years. Thanks for giving me strength and just being there. I love you all.

MY BOYS: Brooklyn, Romeo and Cruz – it's amazing how rips and splodges and the need to turn things inside out because of sicked-up milk can open up a whole range of fashion possibilities. I love you.

DAVID: Your love and support means everything to me. I never thought it was possible but I can honestly say that I love you now more than ever. You complete me and make me who I am.

TO MY FANS: You will never know how much you mean to me. I am so grateful for your loyalty and support. Thank you.

AND A FINAL THANKS TO JOAN COLLINS: For being my real mother.

Love x
Victoria Beckham x
x x

The bed in the Coco Chanel Suite in Paris

Applicator free with purchase

Barbara Cartland eat your heart out

A dirty job but someone has to do it ... (Maria Louise gives me the glitter treatment)

I will have long lashes, I will have long lashes